___ THE ___
SILK PAINTING
WORKSHOP

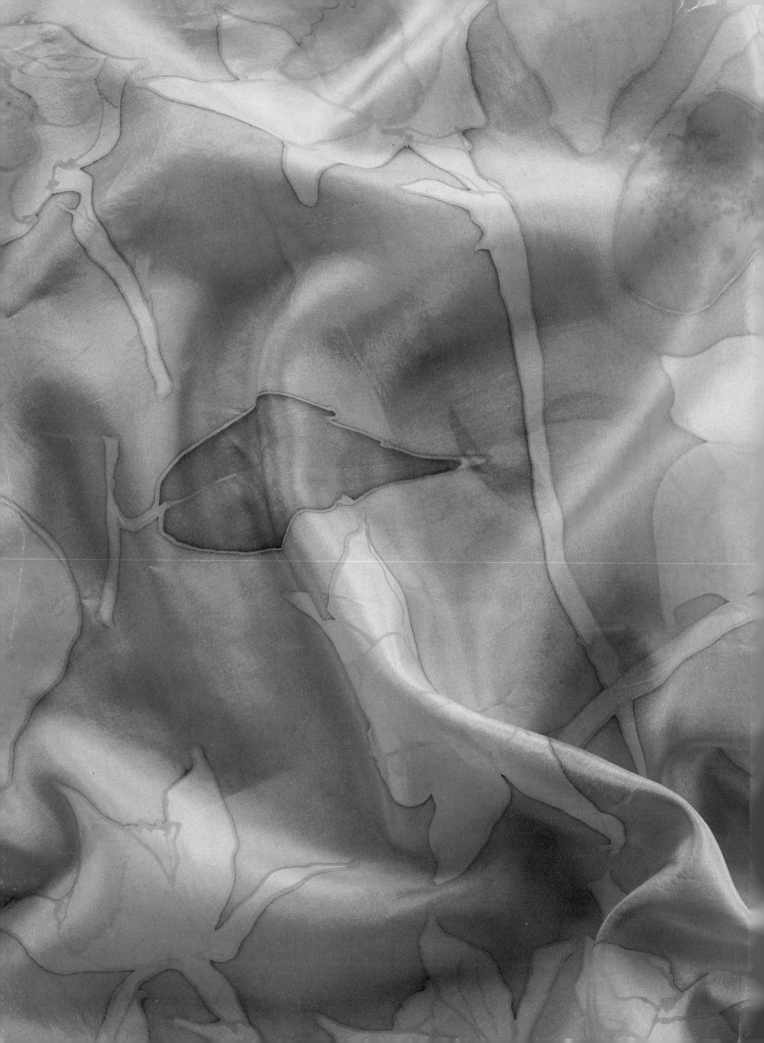

THE
SILK PAINTING
WORKSHOP

Painting, Marbling and Batik for Beginners

JANE VENABLES

David & Charles

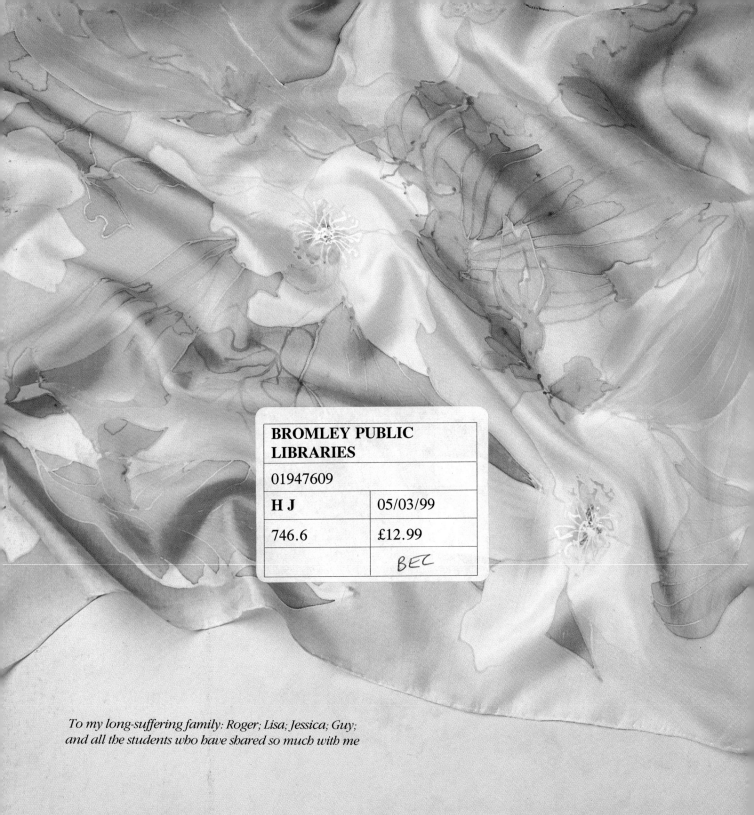

To my long-suffering family: Roger; Lisa; Jessica; Guy;
and all the students who have shared so much with me

Copyright © Jane Venables 1994
(text and illustrations, except where
otherwise attributed)
Copyright © Photography: David & Charles 1994

First published 1994
First published in paperback 1999
Jane Venables has asserted her right to be
identified as author of this work in
accordance with the Copyright, Designs
and Patents Act 1988.

A DAVID & CHARLES BOOK

A catalogue record for this book is
available from the British Library.

ISBN 07153 0933 1

Typeset by ABM Typographics Ltd, Hull
and printed in Italy
by L.E.G.O. SpA
for David & Charles
Brunel House Newton Abbot Devon

CONTENTS

(page 1) *Moon card by Anne Dye
Batiks, a simple use of wax and
merging colours*
(pages 2-3) *Oranges and lemons
scarf, showing the use of salt to
give texture*
(left) *Nevadas and hostas,
showing the use of gutta for
drawing – the white areas are
unpainted*

Introduction

When silk is painted, its surface seems to reflect the colours, giving an added vibrancy. If it is mounted as a picture and viewed from certain angles, the sheen gives a special lustre. The results are beautiful, so there is no wonder that silk painting has become such a popular art form. It is a tranquil relaxing way of painting, which is both creative and rewarding, and anyone with a love of colour should achieve excellent results simply by trying the fabulous dyes and different techniques.

As a craft, silk painting is much easier than it looks. Many people who shy away from drawing with paper and pencil experience an unexpected free-

This rainbow shows the simple use of gutta dividing the complementary colours. Angela Newport's Tree of Life (right) shows the free use of wax with the tjanting

dom and ability to express themselves when using the flowing gutta line, which is the 'pencil' used to draw on silk. Even painting the silk is easy because the dyes are applied to the surface and allowed to flow naturally, allowing the colours to spread softly with wonderful results. If the thought of drawing is still a deterrent, you can always paint an abstract design or geometric pattern – even very simple designs look good on silk. Don't be worried about getting it

wrong either, as failures can often be converted into successes by painting over the colours or, in extreme cases, by washing the silk and starting again! Quite simply it is a highly rewarding way of painting.

This book explains all the basic skills and, once these have been mastered, continues by showing how to experiment with colours, techniques and materials to create quite different results. The key to mastering any craft is gaining confidence, and there are over twenty-five exciting projects, designed to encourage and develop expertise. Complete beginners can follow the comprehensive step-by-step instructions, while more competent painters can use the projects as inspiration.

Everyone will find The Beginner's Paintbox (page 10) invaluable, as it is a detailed guide to the equipment and materials required, from the most suitable silk to the types of dyes and gutta available. The Techniques Workshop (page 16) outlines the many methods used in silk painting, such as gutta, wet-on-dry and Epassisant, and provides practical guidance. When salt is combined with wet dye, for example, fascinating shapes and patterns emerge; these can be used to create the impression of flowers, landscapes or water.

Balancing colours and putting unlikely ones together becomes easier with practice, and Understanding and Using Colour (page 36) explains most of the rules worth knowing, whilst the simple projects show clearly which colours work together and which ones make 'mud'.

Painters are always looking for creative ideas and, whatever your level of ability, there is plenty in this book to stimulate and inspire – from the enchanting floral designs featured in The Four Seasons (page 26),

delightful landscapes and still lifes in The Natural World (page 76), through to colourful patterns in Geometric and Abstract Designs (page 92). It is always helpful to look at the work of others, to see their different styles and observe how they use colour and shape, and throughout there are examples by top silk painters. Other design ideas can be found in Sources of Design (page 64) which discusses how to develop artistic expression and looks at some of

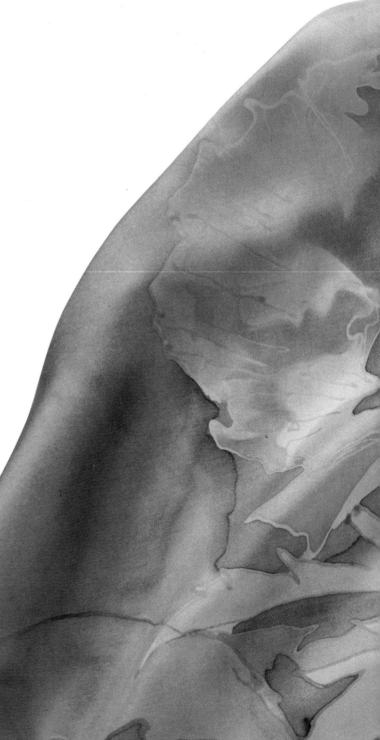

Papaver poppies. *Harmony and softness created by just a few colours intermixed and diluted with water*

the things which may fire your imagination.

Batik and marbling are two crafts which produce excellent designs in their own right, but when combined with silk the finished results are quite exceptional, as can be seen in Batik Effect (page 100) and Marbling (page 110). These chapters list the equipment required for the two techniques and give step-by-step guidance on how to create beautiful results.

Gradually, as your confidence increases, so your own personal style will emerge and, with it, years of pleasure and excitement. There is so much to explore in silk painting, there are always new techniques to try out, colours to mix and effects to create. In fact if it becomes an obsession – as with me – silk painting can be constantly thrilling and absorbing, if a little exhausting!

CHAPTER ONE

The Beginner's Paintbox

Many of the terms and equipment used in silk painting may be unfamiliar to a beginner. The beginner's paintbox is an introduction to much of the terminology and also acts as a reference guide to the equipment required. The specialist equipment listed should be available from good art shops (see Dyes and Suppliers, page 127).

BASIC EQUIPMENT AND MATERIALS

silk

selection of dyes

gutta

plastic pipette with neo-graphic nib No8 or plastic pipette with screw-on nib and wire

frame

masking tape 12mm (½in) wide

silk pins

paintbrushes

water pot(s)

palette

pencil or embroiderer's pen

dropper (for transferring dyes to the palette)

hairdryer (for drying gutta lines and dye)

SILK

To start, use pieces of inexpensive smooth white silk. Silk chiffon, silk georgette, silk satin, silk taffeta and silk twill are all suitable for painting, although one of the best for beginners is habutai. Habutai is a smooth plain white silk which has enough body to hold dye, yet is fine enough for an early hesitant gutta line to penetrate (see opposite). It comes in three weights: fine (5mm, $3/16$in), medium (8mm, $5/16$in) and heavy (10mm, $7/16$in) and two widths: 90cm (35in) and 114cm (44in). Medium-weight habutai is ideal for beginners, and is generally cheaper to buy than the other two, as it is made from standard yarns and weaves. Finer yarns are more expensive to produce as the processing costs are higher, whilst heavier weights, like twill and crêpe, use more silk and different weave structures. Whatever silk is used, always test a small piece of it before painting to see how the dye and gutta penetrate. The cheapest method of buying silk is to obtain it direct from a silk importer (see Dyes and Suppliers, page 127).

If there is any doubt whether a fabric is pure silk, carry out a simple burn test. Light a candle, for safety reasons preferably out of doors, and hold a small piece of the fabric in it. Real silk will not burn well and stops burning as soon as it is removed from the flame. It emits a smell similar to burning wool or feathers and leaves a shiny black residue, which turns into a black powder if crushed between the fingers.

It is virtually impossible to cut a straight line in silk with scissors, because the fabric slides about too much. To get the required size, make a small cut in the silk and tear sharply – a tear follows the grain of the fabric to give a straight line. The silk should be just larger than the inside measurements of the frame (see page 13). Any surplus silk hanging around the frame will just get in the way.

Silk is sensitive to acids, so acid-free card should be used when mounting silk pictures. Exposure to ultra-violet rays found in sunlight also slowly destroys silk filaments so, when framing a silk painting, use protective glass, and never hang a silk painting in direct sunlight.

DYES

These are the colours used to paint silk. They must be mixed with water before application and are very concentrated, so only a small amount is needed. There are many different dyes available, under many different brand names, but the two main types are steam-fixed dyes and iron-fixed dyes. Always buy the same make of dye and gutta. Both types are colour fast after fixing and have double-strength colours available for strong, intense results.

Steam-fixed Dyes

• Dry quickly being spirit-based.
• Give a beautiful, smooth background colour when combined with alcohol (diluant).
• The colours flow easily on silk, spreading with little encouragement.
• If the dyes dry on the palette, a little water can be added, without diluting their strength or intensity.
• Have an extra glow and vibrancy when steamed.
• Work well with salt.
• Can be thickened with Epassisant and controlled with antifusant.
• Must be steam-fixed before washing (see Finishing, page 122).
• Can only be used successfully on pure silk. If used on a silk/cotton mix the results can be paler.

Iron-fixed Dyes

• Quick and easy to use. Just paint on, leave to dry, iron and wash.
• Have their own thickener and antifusant to stop the dyes spreading.
• Work well with salt.
• Can be used on other materials like cotton, linen and some synthetics.
• Difficult to achieve a smooth background over a large area, therefore best used on designs which are divided into small areas.
• Can only be mixed with water, not alcohol, so not very versatile.

• The colours do not flow as easily on silk as steam-fixed dyes.
• Once painted the silk loses some of its softness and lustre.

GUTTA

Gutta is the 'pencil' of silk painting. It draws, it flows and it separates colours. A colourless or metallic liquid with a honey-like consistency, gutta is put into a pipette (see page 12) and gently squeezed onto the silk to form the outlines for the design. When dry these lines separate the colours and stop dyes bleeding into one another. If there is any defect in the lines, such as a gap, dye will force its way through and bleed into the neighbouring colour, often spoiling the end result. Gutta does not become fixed – it washes out after the finished painting has been fixed (except metallic gutta which is usually water-based and needs iron fixing).

There are two types of gutta available, water-based and spirit-based, and both have different uses and qualities. Water-based gutta is easier for a beginner to use, as it does not thicken, either with age or in hot weather. Both types of gutta can be used with iron-fixed and steam-fixed dyes. It is recommended that you use gutta and dye from the same manufacturer.

Water-based Gutta

• Has no smell.
• Washes out easily in warm soapy water after ironing or steaming.
• Never thickens and always retains a good flowing consistency. If a slight lumpiness occurs after colouring, it is too old to use. Throw it away and start afresh.
• Colours easily. Put some in a plastic cup, add a few drops of spirit-based dye (will not work with iron-fixed dyes) to the required colour depth, mix thoroughly and put in a pipette.
• Must be completely dry before painting to be an effective barrier, otherwise the dyes may bleed through the lines. Dry the gutta with a hairdryer before painting.
• If dye is painted over the gutta line it does not form such a strong barrier. Apply dye to either side of the gutta line and allow it to flow up to the line.

To colour water-based gutta, put some in a plastic cup, add a few drops of steam-fixed dye (not iron-fixed) and mix with a spoon. The more drops of colour added, the deeper the final colour

• Some superb metallic guttas are available – remember to iron-fix them before washing.

• Some metallic guttas do not make good barriers as they sit on the surface of the silk rather than penetrating it. Try them out to see how effective they are in holding back dye. You may need to paint the gutta line on both sides of the silk. Alternatively, just use metallic guttas as a decoration rather than for retaining lines.

Spirit-based Gutta

• Forms an excellent barrier.

• Because of the latex content, any dye which accidentally gets on the gutta line will not affect its barrier qualities. This is its greatest advantage.

• Does not have to be completely dry before painting, but acts as a barrier as soon as it is applied. Be careful though: if gutta gets on the paint brush it must be cleaned off with white spirit and warm soapy water before it dries.

• Can thicken in hot weather making it difficult to apply. To stop this happening, keep the pipette in the fridge when not in use or put the gutta back into its own container when you have finished. To thin down thickened gutta add some Essence F (a special thinner) or white spirit, a few drops at a time to the gutta, in a cup, and stir until the gutta returns to its normal honey-like consistency. Pour back into the pipette.

• Not as easy to colour as water-based gutta. Mix about 12mm (½in) of coloured typographic ink (it comes in small tubes) with a little Essence F or white spirit, add to the gutta in a cup and stir well. The depth of colour depends on the amount of ink used.

• Sometimes difficult to remove from the silk if steamed too long. After steaming, soak in white spirit, gently rubbing the lines.

• Has a strong rubbery smell.

PIPETTE

The pipette is a transparent plastic bottle used to hold gutta. The softer the plastic the easier it is to squeeze and expel the gutta. Avoid firm plastic pipettes with little give – although they can be softened by soaking in hot water, they usually harden again.

To apply gutta some instruction leaflets tell you to make a hole in the end of the plastic spout of the pipette and squeeze the gutta out. This often results in a clumsy, uneven line and can destroy a beginner's confidence. Instead put a neo-graphic nib No8 (see illustration) on the pipette, fixing it with masking tape. Although this looks primitive, it works well and should last a long time. The nib can also be removed easily for cleaning. Alternatively, consider a pipette with a screw-on nib and wire (these originated in Germany and France). The wire is used to keep the

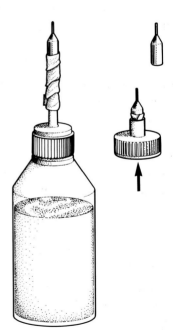

Fix a neo-graphic nib No8 to a pipette of gutta with masking tape – though this looks primitive, it works well

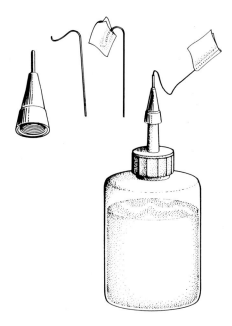

Screw-on nibs come complete with their own pipette and wire. Fix a masking tape marker to the end of the wire so that it does not get lost when it is taken out

fine metal of the nib clear of drying gutta when it is not in use. If the gutta flow seems uneven, push the wire in and out a few times to clear any obstructions. Always leave the wire in the nib when the pipette is not being used. Nibs come in sizes 0.8 (largest) down to 0.4. If the flow is too fast, change to a 0.6.

PENCIL OR EMBROIDERER'S PEN

An ordinary soft 2B pencil can be used to draw designs on silk, although it does not always wash out afterwards. A felt-tipped embroiderer's pen, also known as an invisible pen, is much better as it contains ink that either disappears immediately when touched with water or fades gradually if left (this could be about four days in dry weather, or as quick as four hours if the atmosphere is very damp).

FRAMES

Silk needs to be held firmly and stretched taut so that it can be drawn and painted on freely. For beginners, any square or circle of wood that takes silk pins can be used, an old picture frame or canvas stretchers, for example. Circular embroidery frames are suitable for holding silk when trying out the techniques. As the silk should not touch the work surface during

painting all frames should sit about 75mm (3in) above the table.

Ready-made frames, which can be adapted to different sizes, can be bought from good craft shops. Alternatively, have some made, the most useful sizes are 40, 65 and 90cm (16, 26 and 35in) squares.

MASKING TAPE

Twelve millimetre (½in) wide masking tape is used to cover the edge of the frame (see illustration overleaf) so that dye does not penetrate the wood and then stain the next piece of work. Wipe clean or renew the tape after finishing each piece.

SILK PINS

Always use special three-legged silk pins to fix silk to the frame. They will not mark the silk, unlike drawing pins which break some of the threads and leave a hole. Silk pins simplify the job of painting to the very edge of a piece of silk – necessary when making a scarf – as the fabric is secured with one leg of the pin only, allowing dye to flow underneath.

Always use three-legged silk pins to fix the silk to the frame

PAINTBRUSHES

Try any brush that holds plenty of dye. Chinese paintbrushes are ideal as their points can reach the smallest area whilst the body of the brush holds a great amount of dye. This enables much larger areas to be painted with each brushstroke and gives a smoother result. Ideally, have at hand three different sizes of paintbrush. Special silk painting brushes can be bought at good art and craft shops.

PALETTE AND DROPPER

Initially, transparent egg boxes, or even plates, can be used to mix the dyes, although they must be white or

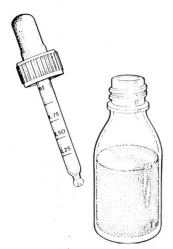

Use a dropper to transfer dye to the palette

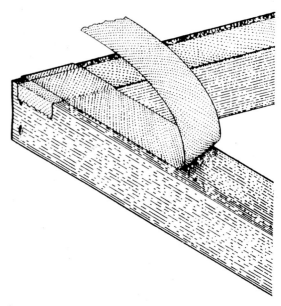

Always put masking tape on the surface of a wooden frame to protect it from dye. If dye gets into the wood it might accidentally be transferred to the next piece of silk and ruin the design

clear. A white plastic palette with areas for mixing the dyes is preferable and available from good art and craft shops. Droppers are essential for transferring dye to the palette, and it is best to use a separate dropper for each dye.

HAIRDRYER
Always have an ordinary hairdryer at hand. It is ideal for drying the gutta lines, and to fix dye to stop it spreading.

FIRST STEPS
Once you have all the equipment, it will need to be prepared before painting starts. Follow these guidelines.

1 Put the nib (size 0.8) onto the pipette (because the makes vary it is best to follow the illustrated instructions on pages 12-13).

2 Fill the pipette with gutta. This is easier if the air in the pipette is squeezed out first. Start pouring in the gutta slowly, releasing the pipette so that it gently draws in the gutta. To prevent the wire from getting lost, fix a marker of masking tape to it (as illustrated).

3 Prepare the frame by putting masking tape along the exposed surfaces (as illustrated). The tape protects the wood from the dyes.

4 To trace a design onto the silk (if you are copying one of the designs featured in The Four Seasons, page 26 for example) place the original on a work surface and fix it in place with pieces of masking tape so that it cannot slip. Lay the silk on top and secure with more tape in the same way. Use an embroiderer's pen or 2B pencil to trace the design onto the silk.

5 Always remove the silk from the work surface and pin it on the frame *before* using gutta. If gutta is applied whilst the silk is still fixed to the work surface, it will penetrate through the fabric and stick to the design.

6 Stretch the silk on the frame so that it is as taut and as smooth as possible. Pin one side, then an adjoining side, ensuring that the grain of the silk is straight. Stretch gently to pin the opposite side as evenly as possible before giving the final side a gentle pull to create a taut, flat surface. Use plenty of pins 40mm (1½in) apart to get the best results.

7 Prepare plenty of clean water in a couple of containers. Not only is the water needed for mixing the dyes – soft, pale colours are achieved by adding water to the dyes – but also for thoroughly rinsing the paintbrushes between colours.

Scattered Flowers by Frannie on pure silk crêpe, using nearly full-strength colours

CHAPTER TWO

Techniques Workshop

Silk painting uses many processes in a variety of ways. Understanding them and how they can be used, gives the confidence to create exciting effects.

Work through the following techniques workshop, copying the designs shown and perhaps experimenting with your own.

EQUIPMENT AND MATERIALS

silk
silk pins
frame covered with masking tape
gutta in pipette
dyes
palette
dropper
Chinese paintbrushes
water pot
paint rag
embroiderer's pen or soft pencil
hairdryer
salt: table, rock and dishwasher salt
alcohol: diluant or surgical spirit (see below)
Epassisant or other thickener (see below)
antifusant (see below)

Before trying out any of the techniques:
- Stretch the silk on the frame using silk pins, as described in 'First Steps', page 14.
- Transfer the dyes to the palette using a dropper.
- Dip the paintbrushes into clean water before loading with dye. Remove the excess water on a paint rag.

WET-ON-DRY/WET-ON-WET

When wet dye is applied over dry, lovely irregular watermarks appear, as shown in the green lines here. Above this, the dark-blue hill merging into the light-blue sky shows the softer line made by wet dye applied on top of wet. This technique is particularly useful in landscapes, as wet-on-dry can emerge looking like rows of trees or mountainous terrains. Wet-on-wet produces beautiful mysterious horizons on land or sea. See the landscape project on page 84.

To copy this example, paint the top half of the silk a soft watery blue, and, whilst still wet, paint a line of dark blue over the bottom section of the pale blue

The effect of wet-on-wet and wet-on-dry

and paint a grey strip below the dark blue. Add some grey areas to the pale-blue sky. Paint the rest of the silk a soft green and leave to dry, or dry with a hair-dryer. To produce the wet-on-dry effects shown, pass a brush of yellow dye over the area where the green and grey meet (the green and grey must be completely dry). To freeze an effect and/or stop a line spreading further, 'fire' a hairdryer at the dye and the image will remain.

WET-ON-DRY CIRCLES

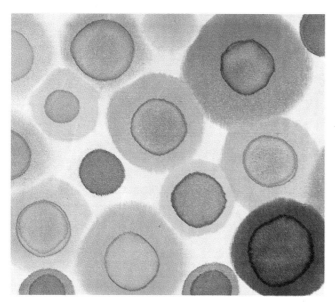

Dropping circles of wet dye onto circles of dry is an attractive way of creating an abstract design

---

This is another way of using wet-on-dry to achieve quite different results. Circles of dye are applied on top of one another, creating very attractive edges. The sizes of the circles are easily controlled by the amount of dye applied, although if a circle is getting too big use a cotton wool bud to absorb any excess dye or 'fire' with a hairdryer to fix it. This is an ideal technique for an all-over scarf design. (See the project on page 42.)

Using six colours (yellow, grey, purple, pink, blue and orange are shown here), apply single circles of dye to the silk, leaving plenty of space between them so that they spread without touching. Leave to dry naturally, or dry with a hairdryer once the circles have grown big enough. When dry, put a drop of

yellow in the centres of the pink, blue and orange circles, then purple in the purple. Leave to dry, or dry with a hairdryer. Apply drops of grey over the purple and orange circles.

WET-MEETING-WET

Lovely patterns can be created using the wet-meeting-wet technique. If wet dyes are applied onto silk they do not mix when they reach one another, but miraculously stop, leaving distinct areas of colour. This is a very useful technique to use when working without gutta. By sprinkling salt in the centre of the circles whilst they are still wet, subtle and interesting variations can be achieved. (See 'Salt' overleaf.) The same technique can be used to paint stripes of colour next to each other (be sure to choose colours that are compatible with one another). (See the project on page 39.)

Choose four colours (yellow, purple, pink and blue are shown here). With the point of a brush, apply drops of one dye randomly over the silk. Repeat with the other three dyes, placing the colours near to each other. As the dyes reach one another they stop, creating this interesting effect.

Put different colours of wet dye onto silk and when they meet they stop, forming lovely soft areas of colour all over the silk

---

SALT

Salt sprinkled onto wet dye produces intriguing results, as the salt attracts the dye and different shapes/patterns emerge. It is an exciting technique because you never quite know what will appear (some colours are more strongly attracted to salt than others), and it is great fun for beginners as it requires no drawing skills. The salt used in this example is dishwasher salt, although rock and table salt can also be used and will give different results. The technique can be used to create many things like flower shapes, landscapes and water. Sometimes, mysterious rock shapes emerge. (See the projects on pages 43–49, and 77.)

Paint a brushful of dye onto your silk and sprinkle on the salt whilst the dye is still wet. If painting a large area, repeat the process as necessary, adding more colour and salt to the silk. (The dye must be very wet for the best results.) Leave the silk to dry *completely* before shaking off the salt. Do not use a hairdryer as this can scatter salt and dye over the work and everywhere else. If this technique is used for flower centres, or other small areas, wait until all the other parts of the design are dry before using salt, as it is hard to confine salt to just one area.

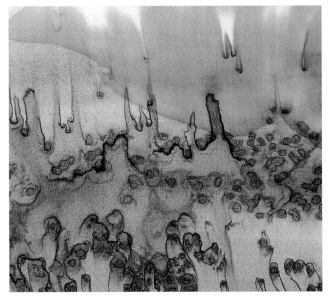

Salt sprinkled on wet dye draws up the colour and creates interesting shapes

ALCOHOL OR DILUANT

Drops of alcohol applied onto dry dye give these lovely shapes as the dye is dispersed by the spirit – stripes, zig-zags and other patterns can be produced with this technique. The alcohol used in silk painting is called diluant and is available at good craft shops, although surgical spirit will create equally interesting effects. They can only be used with steam-fixed dyes, not iron-fixed ones.

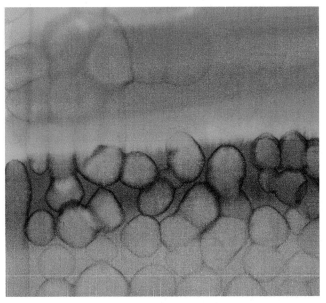

Alcohol dropped onto dry dye forms intriguing asymmetrical shapes

To produce the effect shown, first paint the silk with stripes of colour and leave to dry. Dip a brush into the alcohol (diluant) and, using just the point, gently touch the silk, allowing the alcohol (diluant) to form a small circle. Repeat this process all over the required area. To create other shapes, dip the point of the brush in alcohol (diluant) and paint straight lines to create stripes, zig-zags, curves or whatever.

Because it is difficult to get an even spread of dye over a large area, especially with pale colours, alcohol (diluant) can also be used to dilute background colours to achieve a more even result. Diluting the dye with alcohol (diluant) *instead of water*, prevents the background becoming blotchy, and gives a wonderfully even result. (See the project on page 59.)

GUTTA

Gutta is the transparent, colourless outliner which keeps one dye from spreading into another when painting on silk. It should be the consistency of honey and is applied with a special pipette designed to dispense a smooth even flow – although this needs practice to be perfect. The two types of gutta available (spirit-based and water-based) and their advantages and disadvantages are covered in detail on pages 11–12.

Lines painted with gutta appear white as the paint cannot penetrate the silk, but if there is a fault in the gutta line (such as a gap), the dyes may bleed into one another. Metallic and coloured guttas are available and colourless gutta can be coloured, giving a variety of options for drawing.

The bold use of colourless gutta can be clearly seen on this example, as it was used to 'draw' the outline of the petals and the flower centre. Metallic gutta was added to create the centre petals. Deep pink and blue dyes were applied to the petals and around the background, using the wet-on-wet-technique. More examples are shown in 'Working With Colour and Gutta', page 50.

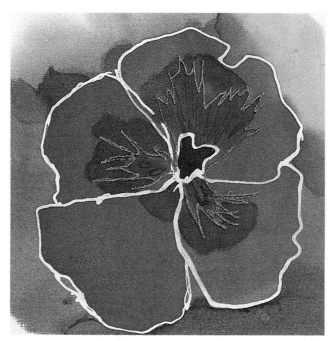

Gutta, the pencil used to 'draw' on silk, forms a barrier to keep the colours spreading into one another. The colourless outliner appears white, as dye is unable to penetrate the silk where it is used

THICKENER OR EPASSISANT

Epassisant is a transparent glue-like thickener which is mixed with the dyes. When this mixture is applied to the silk it does not penetrate the fabric, but hangs suspended in lovely gradations of tone as seen here. This makes it useful for painting flowers and land-scapes, as it is impossible to achieve a smooth effect. It makes the silk feel stiff when it has dried, but washes out after fixing. (See the project on page 34.)

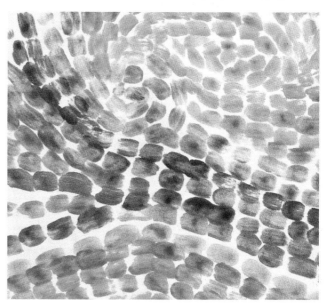

Epassisant is a thickener mixed with dyes to prevent them bleeding into the silk. The colour remains on the surface of the silk

Each dye manufacturer produces their own thickener, and it is always best to stick to the same make for both dye and thickener. (Epassisant is the name of Dupont's thickener.) Alternatively, make your own by mixing Manutex, a powdered seaweed available from good craft shops, with water.

Sprinkle one teaspoon of powder onto 150ml (¼pt) of cold water, stir and leave to thicken. Mix a little on the palette with some dye. Home-made thickeners can be used with most dyes, although it is always advisable to test them out first before using on a specific design.

To create the effect shown, on the palette mix thickener or Epassisant, a little water and some dyes (pink, purple, blue and green were used here). The mixture should be of a honey-like consistency. Paint the lines on the silk in gentle, sweeping strokes. The shading appears as the thickened paint is applied and remains suspended as it dries.

ANTIFUSANT

Antifusant is a transparent liquid which prevents dye spreading. It is painted onto the silk in the area(s) required and dried with a hairdryer, the design is then painted over it and the dye stays in place. It can be used to paint in parts of a landscape, like a delicate network of branches, flower stalks and grasses, and is particularly suitable where extremely fine details are required. It will not leave watermarks if painted over areas of unfixed colour.

Useful though it is, this is not a medium to be over-

When antifusant is painted over silk, it stops the dye spreading, allowing extremely fine details to be added to a design

used because, once it has dried, the silk becomes crackly like paper and you lose the essential qualities of the silk. Washing does not remove it entirely.

Antifusant is available from craft shops, although you can make your own from one part gutta to six parts solvent (such as Essence F or white spirit). This home-made version is useful if the commercially produced antifusant is not available. It is also cheaper, but it may leave watermarks if used over unfixed dyes.

In this example, a piece of silk has been painted with antifusant and a leaf design painted over it, resulting in a soft, slightly fuzzy edge (unlike the hard definite line you would get with gutta). Antifusant can also be coloured and painted onto silk, a technique used on the bamboo leaves shown here.

BACKGROUNDS

The background colour is an integral part of any design and should be carefully chosen. Sometimes it is appropriate to leave the background white, as shown in the sweet-pea scarf (below). At other times a painted background is better. The colour chart on page 38 provides help in deciding which colours work best together, but always consider the main subject of the design and the intended finished effect. Warm rich colours can change a picture totally, as seen in the hot brilliant colours of the orange vase of flowers set against an orange cloth (opposite). This hot look was offset by painting the background a blue/grey, which has the effect of 'cooling down' the

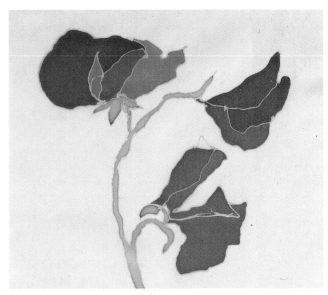

(Above) The choice of background colour is integral to any design, white being highly effective for these sweet peas

(Right) Exercise caution when choosing a background colour for richly coloured designs such as this brilliant-orange vase of flowers

picture. Without it, the final effect would have appeared blisteringly hot.

Generally, it is always better to leave the background until last, when there is a better idea of what colour (and how deep a colour) to use to pull the whole design together. The only exception is when a certain pale colour has been decided on in advance, in which case it can be applied before the design is drawn on. Leaving the background till last also means any gaps which have appeared in the gutta can be repaired and another leaf, for example, may be added. When making the butterfly cushions (opposite) the gutta was very weak and the colours bled through the lines a great deal. In the end, the gutta was repaired and the background painted black, which covered all the inaccuracies – a desperate measure that worked!

Always mix enough background colour to complete the whole area as it is almost impossible to match colours exactly, and there will be a watermark problem where the first area has dried. Approximately 4 tbsp made-up dye will cover a scarf 1m (39in) square.

Diluant Background

So many people I know, and beginners in particular, have problems painting a smooth even background over a large area. They usually get an uneven blotchy result. But there is a solution if steam-fixed dyes are used. Mix a dye with alcohol (diluant) only, instead of water (iron-fixed dyes will not mix with diluant). As there is no water to run out of the dye as it is painted on the silk, a more even colour is achieved. However, the dye-loaded brush must be applied firmly and evenly in all directions over the silk to ensure that the colour penetrates, and to avoid any brush strokes showing. When painting a background, do not allow any part of it to dry, otherwise watermarks will form.

Sometimes a background colour can hide inaccuracies. The gutta of this design was so weak that the dyes bled through. After repairing the gutta, the background was painted black to cover the dyes which had bled

A soft wet or dry background can be very effective, particularly with floral designs

Interesting Background

A soft wet or dry background can be very effective behind flowers, for example in the iris picture (above). Soft stripes of grey and turquoise were painted behind the flower, two broad leaves were added in gutta on the coloured area and dried. As the gutta was applied on a colour, it does not appear white but takes on the base colour – a good way of avoiding white gutta lines. Deep blue and turquoise leaf shapes were painted onto the background and, as the brush strokes were the shapes of the leaves, they formed their own soft watermarked edge.

Breaking Up Backgrounds

Sometimes a more even result is achieved if the background is broken up into several smaller areas, as seen in the artichoke scarf (below). The artichokes were drawn and painted first, then the leaves were added all over the silk, disappearing over the edge to break up the background. The border was drawn and painted purple, the background painted green and, finally, silver gutta leaf shapes were scattered over the design.

Using Salt

Another method which gives very interesting effects is to sprinkle a few granules of salt, very sparingly, over a painted background. As the salt draws up the wet dye it can look very attractive. Applying a little salt is often more effective than if it had been sprinkled on liberally.

Some designs lend themselves to broken backgrounds, as on this artichoke scarf

BORDERS

Creating a separate border is one way of finishing off a design and is particularly effective when painting a silk scarf.

The first thing is to decide how wide a border is required and then mark this measurement on the silk. To do this, cut out a square of card the same size as the border, for example if the border is going to be 5cm (2in) cut out a 5cm (2in) square. Stretch the silk on the frame using the silk pins, as described on page 13. Place the card square in one corner of the fabric and mark on the corner with an embroiderer's pen. Move the square along about 15cm (6in) and mark on the width of the border with dots, then continue all the way round the fabric.

It is much easier to draw on the border design

using this dot method rather than a ruler line, just keep the next dot visible out of the corner of your eye as you gutta. It is also a much better technique to employ if the border is to be marked with a straight line, as it is much more difficult to follow a drawn line with gutta than to draw one freehand. It does not matter if the line is slightly uneven. This adds to the hand work and gives a more sensitive result.

Working a gutta line freehand can be very satisfactory, but may seem daunting. Have heart, face the border, start in one corner, take a deep breath, start squeezing and 'draw'. Try not to stop until the next corner is reached, any gaps can always be repaired. Turn the frame round 90° and continue. Try to control the drawing elbow by holding it rigid at your side as you work – you find yourself holding your breath

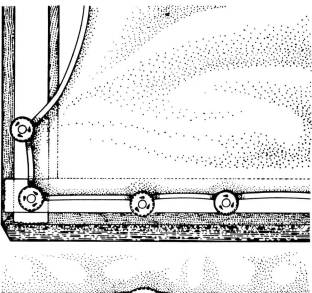

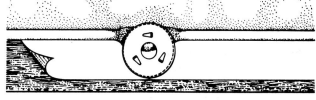

Pin the edge of a scarf to the frame using one leg of the silk pin to hold it. This way dye goes right to the edge, leaving no white marks

whilst working, but that is quite normal, and it seems to help the concentration!

If a ruled gutta line is essential, place the ruler upside-down, so that the edge is off the silk. Rest the pipette nib against the ruler at an angle as you 'draw', to stop gutta touching the ruler's edge. If the ruler is long enough for the gutta line to be applied in one stroke all the better.

The trick when painting any border design is to prevent a dry line forming, which could spoil the overall effect. Always make sure enough of the right colour(s) is mixed up before starting – stopping midway through painting to try to create the same colour can cause problems. To avoid wet-on-dry marks, first paint the top edge from left to right, then the two sides, painting from top to bottom, finally the bottom edge, painting from left to right.

When painting the border of a scarf, pin the edges to the frame as shown (above) using just one leg of the silk pins to hold it. Pinned in this way the dye goes right up to the edges and leaves no white marks.

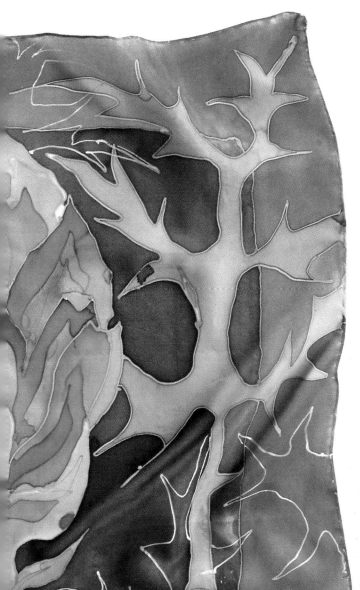

CHAPTER THREE

The Four Seasons

The four floral designs featured in this chapter depict the four seasons. They make excellent first projects for a newcomer to silk painting, as the designs can either be traced onto the silk or drawn freehand.

SNOWDROPS

This is an excellent project for anyone new to using the gutta technique. Snowdrops and aconites have crisp simple shapes and clear colours, which are reflected by the simplicity of the design and accentuated by the use of three colours: grey, green and yellow. The gutta outlines remain white, as do the areas which are left unpainted.

YOU WILL NEED

habutai silk

masking tape

embroiderer's pen or soft pencil

frame

silk pins

pipette of water-based gutta

hairdryer

dyes: yellow, green and grey

palette

dropper

Chinese paintbrush

water pot

paint rag

cotton wool buds

alcohol (diluant)

1 The first step is to transfer the design onto the silk. This can be done in one of three ways:
• Tape the paper design onto the work surface and lay the silk on top, taping it in place. Trace off the design using an embroiderer's pen or soft pencil. Fix the silk onto the frame, which should be protected with masking tape as described on page 14.
• Or, stretch the silk onto the protected frame, as described on page 14, put the paper design underneath, raising it with a book or piece of foam so it is clearly visible through the silk. Trace off the design using an embroiderer's pen or soft pencil.
• Or, stretch the silk onto the protected frame, as described on page 14, turn over the frame and place it on top of the paper design. Trace off the design using an embroiderer's pen or soft pencil so that the design appears in reverse on the right side of the silk. Leave it like this or unpin the silk and fix it back to the frame the right way.
2 The next step is to outline with gutta. Before starting, ensure the silk is suspended on the frame, clear of the work surface. Check that the gutta is the consistency of honey and flows out of the pipette smoothly.
3 Remove the wire from the pipette nib and squeeze the bottle gently, touching the silk with the nib until a continuous, even line emerges. (Try this out on newspaper first to acquire the knack and gain confidence – the correct flow and pressure comes with practice.) Start to copy the design onto the silk, smoothly following the lines.

Snowdrops is an excellent project for newcomers to the gutta technique

When the pipette is not in use put the wire back into the nib and rest the pipette at an angle (see illustration) so that the air bubble is at the bottom and not at the nib end. If a bubble of air passes through the nib it can cause the gutta line to break.

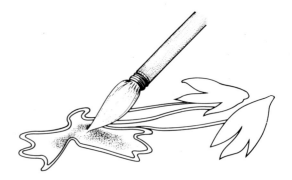

Do not paint every part of a design, simply touch the silk with the tip of the brush and the dye spreads naturally to the edge of the gutta outlines

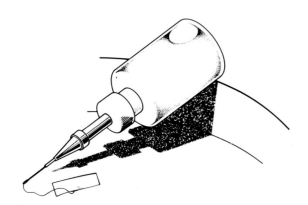

When a pipette of gutta is not being used, always keep the wire inserted and rest the pipette at an angle, so that any air bubbles stay at the bottom. An air bubble in the gutta line causes a break

Frequently check that the gutta line is unbroken by holding up the work to the light. A good, smooth line will appear unbroken and transparent, if it is grey the gutta has not penetrated the silk. Work on the lines, repairing any breaks with a little more gutta. Take care though: too thick a gutta line looks clumsy and takes time to dry, and dye can leak through a line that is too thin.

4 Leave to dry thoroughly – about 30 minutes – or use a hairdryer. Touch the gutta to make sure it is not tacky. Once it has dried completely, you are ready to start painting.

5 Transfer the dyes to separate sections of the palette using a dropper or brush (washed clean between each colour).

6 Dip a brush in clean water and load with yellow. If using a Chinese paintbrush, press it gently on a paint rag before loading with dye to remove the excess water – too much water makes the colour very watery and pale.

7 With the point of the brush, paint the aconite petals. Do not 'paint' every part, just apply the dye centrally to the required areas with the tip of the brush, allowing colour to flow freely up to the gutta lines. Do not

paint near the gutta or put too much dye on the brush or the gutta barrier may break. Use a cotton wool bud to remove excess dye. If the colour is too pale, add a little more dye to the tip of the brush.

8 One of the joys of gutta is that the dyes can be painted on one after another without waiting for each one to dry. So, rinse the brush clean, dip into the green, add some water and a little yellow to make the colour come alive – or mix to create an attractive colour – and paint the aconite leaves using the technique described in step 7. Rinse the brush clean.

9 Transfer more green to the palette, add water and a little grey and mix to give a green/grey. Paint the snowdrop leaves using the technique described in step 7. The snowdrop flowers are the natural white of the silk.

10 Make enough grey to cover the background, by mixing two teaspoons of dye with alcohol (diluant). To find out if it is the right depth of colour, put a drop on the edge of the silk and dry with a hairdryer. Add more dye or alcohol as required.

11 With a clean brush, paint over the entire background in one go; do not allow the dye to dry or watermarks may appear. Rinse the brush clean.

12 Whilst the background is still wet, paint a pale green around the aconite flowers to create a soft watery shadow. Rinse the brush clean.

13 Add grey to the centre of the aconite flowers to give depth. Add a little grey to the white snowdrops to give the impression of shadows. Leave to dry.

14 Steam or iron, depending on the dyes. Wash, following the instructions given in 'Finishing', page 122.

THE WILD ROSE

The shape of the wild rose (overleaf) has always interested me. Its petals have flowing lines and the positive centre makes it well suited to silk painting. Unlike 'Snowdrops', where nearly all of the design is outlined with gutta, this design is less precise and has a much softer 'painted' feel, the result of using coloured gutta for most of the outlines.

YOU WILL NEED

habutai silk

frame covered with masking tape

silk pins

embroiderer's pen or soft pencil

two pipettes of colourless, water-based gutta

plastic cup and spoon (to mix gutta)

steam-fixed dyes: green, brown, pink, yellow, blue and grey

pipette of Javana metallic gutta (copper coloured)

palette

dropper

Chinese paintbrush

water pot

paint rag

cotton wool buds

salt

hairdryer

gold and grey gutta (optional)

Detail of Wild Rose

1 Trace the design onto the silk using one of the methods described for 'Snowdrops', page 26. Stretch the silk onto the protected frame using silk pins, as described on page 14.

2 Using a pipette of water-based gutta, outline the two roses and their centres. Check that the lines are unbroken, repairing any gaps. Leave to dry.

3 Empty the second pipette of water-based gutta into a plastic cup. Add four or five drops of green and mix thoroughly with a spoon. Pour back into the empty pipette. (Spirit-based gutta cannot be coloured in this way, nor can iron–fixed dyes be used. Only steam-fixed dyes mix with water-based gutta.)

4 Using the green gutta, outline the rosebud and leaves.

5 Using the Javana metallic copper gutta, outline the twigs. (Alternatively, colour some water-based gutta brown, following the same procedure described in step 3.) Leave to dry.

6 Transfer dyes to separate sections of the palette using a dropper or brush – wash between each colour.

7 Dip a small brush in clean water, remove the excess on a paint rag, load with brown and carefully paint the twigs. Rinse the brush clean.

8 Load brush with green and paint the leaves. Mix some yellow with the green, paint the bud sepals. Rinse the brush clean.

9 Load brush with pink and paint the bud and some of the rose petals. Creating a pale pink by dipping a watery brush into the pink, paint some more petals. Mix yellow with pink to create a slightly different shade and paint the remaining petals.

10 On the palette make up some pale blue, pale grey and yellow/green for the background.

11 Paint the background, one colour at a time, allowing the colours to spread and merge. Leave to dry.

12 Add slightly stronger tones of grey and green on top of the background to the left of the roses to give a lovely cloudy watermarked effect.

13 Create the flower centres by painting on yellow then immediately adding a little salt. The salt draws up the colour into interesting textures similar to the centre of a flower. Leave to dry.

14 Using gold and grey gutta (optional), add dots of colour for the stamens.

15 Steam and wash, following the instructions given in 'Finishing', page 122. After washing, the gutta will be washed out, although the green dye it was mixed with remains, creating a green line which adds to the finished effect.

THE WILD POPPY

Wild poppies blow freely in the wind and this design (overleaf) tries to capture that mood, so it should be painted with more freedom than the previous two. The secret is to try to draw some of the design freehand, rather than copying it slavishly from the original. The background uses the wet-on-wet and wet-on-dry techniques, whilst the design itself is created using coloured gutta and by retaining white areas of silk with spirit gutta. This project shows how useful spirit gutta is in a 'free' design, where colour can be painted over the top. Water-based gutta would take on the colours painted over it.

The Wild Rose is a soft design created using both colourless and coloured gutta

Detail of Wild Poppy

YOU WILL NEED

habutai silk

soft pencil

frame covered with masking tape

silk pins

pipette of colourless, water-based gutta

plastic cup and spoon (to mix gutta)

dyes: red, yellow, blue, grey, pink and orange

pipette of spirit-based gutta

palette

dropper

Chinese paintbrush

water pot

paint rag

cotton wool buds

hairdryer

grey metallic gutta

1 Trace the poppies, barley and some of the white flowers of the design onto the silk using a soft pencil.

2 Stretch the silk onto the protected frame using silk pins, as described on page 14.

3 Colour the pipette of water-based gutta red, following the procedure described in step 3 of 'The Wild Rose'.

4 Using the red gutta, outline the poppy petals and bud.

5 Using the spirit-based gutta, outline the white dead-nettle flowers and camomile flowers, including the outlines for the yellow centres.

6 Transfer dyes to separate sections of the palette using a dropper or brush – wash clean between each colour.

7 Dip a brush in clean water, remove the excess on a paint rag, load with soft yellow and paint the top of the background behind the poppies.

8 Without washing the brush, dip it into the blue to make a green and use this colour to paint around the

The Wild Poppy should have the feel of flowers blowing in the wind. The design is gradually built up by drawing and painting part of the design, then drawing and painting more details, until it is finally completed

poppies. Continue on creating shades of green, by adding grey or yellow, and painting small areas of the background, gradually working down to the bottom of the design.

9 Paint the area around the dead nettles shades of soft blue/grey. At the bottom finish with the same yellow used at the top: this helps balance the barley. This wet-on-wet technique is effective, as the wet colours all merge giving a soft background, which is ready to be worked on again.

10 Rinse the brush clean and paint the poppies using red, pink and orange. The petals of real poppies have many different colours, so do not paint these petals in one flat colour but mix the colours together to give different shades. Leave to dry.

11 When the background is completely dry, use the spirit-based gutta to trace over the pencil lines and outline the barley, dead-nettle leaves, camomile leaves and poppy buds and stems. Work freely. The stems can be sketchy as they will remain paler when painted over with more colour. Aim for a tangled undergrowth look. Because the background has been completely coloured these gutta lines will not be white after washing, but will stay the colour of what is underneath them.

12 Dry the gutta with a hairdryer then strengthen the colours within the leaf outlines and the barley. Make the camomile leaves around the base of the poppies a vibrant green/yellow, the dead-nettle leaves to the left of the design a blue/green. Keep dye out of the white flowers. Add more gutta stems and leaves over the newly applied colours.

13 Carry on drawing with gutta, drying, adding more colour and drying.

14 Strengthen the colour of the poppy buds and the background around the barley, and elsewhere if necessary. Paint the centres of the camomile flowers yellow. Forget precision painting, as flowing colour and watermarks will add to the effect.

15 Use grey metallic gutta to dot in the poppy centres, then add any other details, like the poppy stems. Leave to dry.

16 Steam and wash, following the instructions given in 'Finishing', page 122. The result should be like a watercolour painting with the poppies and white flowers shining out of a hedgerow.

HOLLY AND MISTLETOE

The sheer whiteness of the Christmas rose and mistletoe berries are set off by the steel-grey background, whilst the green leaves and red holly berries provide welcome pools of colour. This project uses another technique, Epassant – described in more detail on page 19 – together with plain and coloured gutta.

YOU WILL NEED

habutai silk

frame covered with masking tape

silk pins

embroiderer's pen or soft pencil

pipette of colourless, water-based gutta

pipette of red, water-based gutta

two pipettes of green, water-based gutta: one green/blue, one green/yellow

palette

dropper

steam-fixed dyes: green, blue, red, yellow and grey

Chinese paintbrush

Epassisant

water pot

paint rag

cotton wool buds

pipette of gold gutta

hairdryer

1 Trace the design onto the silk using one of the methods described in 'Snowdrops', page 26. Stretch the silk onto the protected frame using silk pins, as described on page 14.
2 Using the colourless gutta, outline the Christmas rose and mistletoe berries.
3 Using the red gutta, outline some of the holly berries.

4 Using the green/blue gutta, outline all the holly leaves and draw in veins on the leaves to the right of the design.
5 Using the green/yellow gutta, outline the mistletoe leaves and stalks and draw in some of the finer details. Leave to dry.
6 Transfer green and blue dye to the palette using a dropper or brush, put a little Epassisant on the palette and mix in some green and blue.
7 Use this mixed colour to paint all the holly leaves on the left of the design. The colour is not absorbed by the silk but stays suspended on top in the shape of the holly leaves.
8 Transfer some red dye to the palette, add a little Epassisant and mix well. Use this to paint on some holly berries. Epassisant affects the sheen of silk, so always use it sparingly otherwise you will lose the wonderful merging of colours and the soft mysterious effect which silk gives.
9 Transfer green, yellow and grey dyes to the palette. Rinse the brush clean, mix together some green and grey and paint the remaining holly leaves. Rinse the brush clean.
10 Mix together some green and yellow and paint the mistletoe leaves and stems. Rinse the brush clean.
11 Transfer grey to the palette and use to paint the background. Start with a pale watery grey then add more colour to make it darker, so that the strongest contrast is around the white Christmas rose. The deeper the background colour behind the rose the more amazing the whites will appear. The Epassisant-painted leaves do not readily hold back dye, so use only a small amount of colour on the brush and carefully apply the grey round the leaves.
12 Mix a little grey and green/yellow with Epassisant and use to carefully shade the Christmas rose. Mix a little green with Epassisant and dab on to create the rose centre.
13 Add fine lines and dots of gold gutta for the stamens. Leave to dry.
14 Steam and wash, following the instructions given in 'Finishing', page 122.

Holly and Mistletoe *is a striking design of contrasts, which uses gutta and Epassisant to great effect*

CHAPTER FOUR
Understanding and Using Colour

Many people are hesitant about colour, but don't let this be a problem. Mixing colours and putting together different combinations, gives the confidence and knowledge needed to use colour successfully.

Unlike watercolours, silk dyes tend to affect the colours they are painted over in different ways. For example, they can displace them, disperse the darker colours to the edge of the gutta shape, or mix with them – the effect is always unexpected. The likely reactions can only be learnt through trial and error, by using the dyes and trying out the possible combinations. Spirit-based yellow is particularly volatile, fiercely sending colours to other areas – similar to the effect alcohol has when painted onto a coloured area – and often with unexpected results.

COLOUR COMBINATIONS

'What colours go together?' is a question that worries a lot of people. And with silk painting, just like any other form of painting, making the right choice is important to the end result. Just take a look at a herbaceous border, which might combine orange with purple, blue with green, whilst red, violet, pink and orange are seen all together and all harmonise. In other words, the most unlikely combinations do work well together and can look quite spectacular, just be adventurous and try them out.

Mixing colours for silk painting is exciting and liberating, and the results can be both surprising and rewarding. Put together emerald and hot pink to make purple and the result is vibrant purple – and I mean vibrant! The colour glows and shimmers, adding another dimension to the silk after it has been steamed. Balancing colours and putting unlikely ones together does become easier with practice, but the first step is to learn a few rules about the silk dyes.

- Blue and yellow make green.
- Blue and pinky-red make purple.
- Yellow and red or pink make orange.
- Purple and green make grey. A created grey made from various strengths of purple and different greens gives a variety of hues and tends to be more 'alive' than a ready-made one.
- Red and green make mud! As do many other combinations.

Because so many silk dyes are available, try to get to know a small selection of colours with all their tones thoroughly before buying a full range. To begin, buy two reds, one blue and two yellows. One of the reds should be red/blue to mix with blue to make purple; the other red should be a clear bright red to mix with yellow to make orange. One of the yellows should be lemon yellow to mix with blue to give a sharp green; the other should be yolk yellow, which is richer in colour, to mix with blue to give a mellow green. Paint each colour on a piece of silk, mix the colours together on the palette and paint the mixed colours on the silk. Keep the painted silk for reference.

PRIMARY, SECONDARY AND TERTIARY COLOURS

Not everyone has a natural colour sense, although colour sense is something which can be learnt, and

If you mix a primary colour with a secondary colour the result is called a *tertiary*.

PRIMARY		SECONDARY		TERTIARY
Red	+	orange	=	red/orange
Yellow	+	orange	=	yellow/orange
Yellow	+	green	=	yellow/green
Blue	+	green	=	blue/green
Blue	+	violet	=	blue/violet
Red	+	violet	=	red/violet

The best way of seeing this visually is to paint the colours on silk. On a length of silk, use the silk dyes to paint a stripe of each primary colour – one red, one yellow and one blue – leaving white gaps between them. Mix together some red and yellow to make orange, then paint this between the red and yellow. The orange is the *secondary* colour.

Mix a little orange with some red and paint this between the orange and red. Mix some orange with a little yellow and paint this between the orange and yellow. The red/orange and yellow/orange are the *tertiary* colours.

Continue this process. Mix the blue and yellow to make green, and paint it between the blue and yellow on the silk. Mix the green with a little yellow, and paint this between the yellow and green. Mix the green with a little blue, and paint it between the blue and green. Finish by mixing blue and red to make violet, then mix some violet with blue and some with red, and paint in the appropriate gaps. You now have the complete range.

COMPLEMENTARY COLOURS

The range of colour combinations is infinite and exciting and when painting there are times when a colour that complements existing colours is needed, when choosing a background colour, for example. There are two options in this situation: colours which create a strong contrast and vibrancy, or colours which are harmonious and closely related. The ladder of complementary colours and the colour wheel show how this works.

The ladder of complementary colours. Painting the primary, secondary and tertiary colours is an excellent way of seeing how they relate to one another

understanding the relationship between primary, secondary and tertiary colours (words used to describe colour) does help.

There are three *primary* colours: red, yellow and blue. They are known as primary because all other colours are made from them. Each one mixes with one of the other two to make three other colours: orange, green and violet, the *secondary* colours.

PRIMARY				SECONDARY
Red	+	yellow	=	orange
Yellow	+	blue	=	green
Blue	+	red	=	violet

STRONGEST CONTRASTS

RED (Primary)	v	GREEN (Secondary)
RED/VIOLET (Tertiary)	v	YELLOW/GREEN (Tertiary)
VIOLET (Secondary)	v	YELLOW (Primary)
BLUE/VIOLET (Tertiary)	v	YELLOW/ORANGE (Tertiary)
BLUE (Primary)	v	ORANGE (Secondary)
BLUE/GREEN (Tertiary)	v	RED/ORANGE (Tertiary)
GREEN (Secondary)	v	RED (Primary)

The Ladder of Complementary Colours

The colour family starts with the three primary colours: red, blue and yellow. Mix any two to get a secondary colour, mix a primary and a secondary to get a tertiary and so the colour family grows. Arranging the primary, secondary and tertiary colours on a ladder (page 37) shows which ones in the group have the greatest contrast and vibrancy to each other, in other words are *complementary*. The colours with the strongest contrasts are those which do not have a common base colour.

Harmonious or *related* colours, on the other hand, are those which have a common base colour and are found next to each other on the ladder, for example red and red/violet.

The Colour Wheel

The colour wheel is another way of showing how to find complementary colours. Divide a circle into twelve segments. Put the three primary colours in segments one (red), five (blue) and nine (yellow), the three secondary colours in segments three (violet), seven (green) and eleven (orange) and the six tertiary colours in segments two (red/violet), four (blue/violet), six (blue/green), eight (yellow/green), ten (yellow/orange) and twelve (red/orange). The colours directly opposite one another on the colour wheel are the ones with the strongest contrast. The ones next to each other are related and are the most harmonious.

Although contrasting colours look effective when used against one another, do not attempt to mix

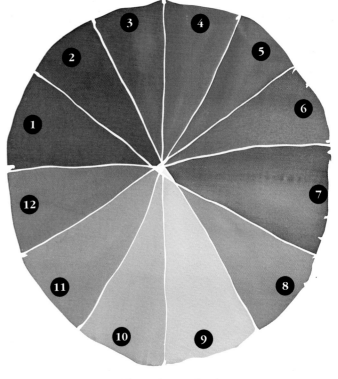

The Colour Wheel

them. Mixing any colours opposite one another on the colour wheel results in mud! A glorious red can turn very jaded when green is put over it. Try it yourself. Put a little of the three primary colours onto the palette, then start mixing. First, mix the secondary then the tertiary colours, then mix contrasting colours. The clear colour sections of the palette will slowly become muddier and muddier.

It is only by using colours, by experimenting with them and understanding what can and cannot be done, that colour sense develops. In time choosing colours for silk painting which are clear, exciting and harmonious becomes second nature.

If possible, keep the silk samples together as a reminder of what colours work and what do not. They will be invaluable as a colour reference guide. Because acid rots silk, keep the samples in a book of acid-free paper which can be bought at art shops. For the same reason all silk pictures should be mounted on acid-free card.

TARTAN SCARF

This project (overleaf) looks very effective, but does take some thought. It is the result of painting different coloured stripes across the silk and across each other. Try it a few times and do not worry if some of your experiments create mud colours! This is an effective and visual way of learning the range of colours which can be created with silk dyes.

YOU WILL NEED

masking tape

frame

silk square of any size

silk pins

dyes: yellow, blue, pink, emerald and red

palette

dropper

four Chinese paintbrushes, one for each colour

water pot

paint rag

hairdryer

1 Put masking tape on the frame and stretch on the silk using silk pins, as described on page 14.
2 Transfer dyes to separate sections of the palette using a dropper or brush (wash dropper or brush clean between each colour).

First paint the silk with stripes of yellow dye.

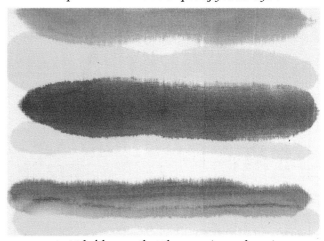

. . . next apply blue, so that the merging colour is green, apply pink . . .

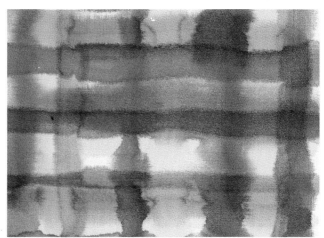

. . . turn the frame and add more stripes across the ones you have just painted, adding emerald and red

Avoid putting together colours that will create 'mud', for example, paint red over yellow and blue, but not over green

39

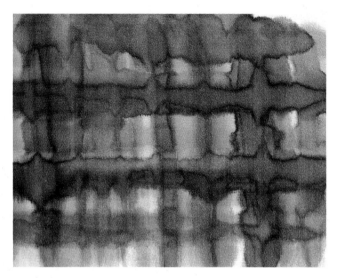

A muddy result is produced if unrelated colours are used together

3 Load a clean brush with yellow, add a little water and paint three well-spaced lines across the silk. Initially, apply just the point of the brush, gradually increasing the pressure as it is moved across the fabric. This prevents too much colour being applied in one spot and should result in an even line across the silk. It also avoids the need to reload the brush halfway across.

4 Paint three blue stripes in the same way, just touching the yellow ones so that the merging colour is green.

5 Paint three pink stripes next to the blue ones, just touching so that the merging colour is purple.

6 Dry with a hairdryer.

7 Turn the frame a quarter of the way round

This tartan scarf looks stunning, and is a useful way of learning which colours work with one another and which ones make 'mud'

(through 90°) and paint coloured stripes across the ones already painted, using the same colours, method and order. Dry with a hairdryer. The wet-on-dry lines formed where the colours cross give unexpected results and colours.

8 Turn the frame a quarter of the way round again (through 90°), ready to paint more stripes. At this stage feel free to introduce other colours, such as emerald and red. The aim is to paint over colours that will produce harmonising shades whilst leaving parts of all the colour stripes showing. *Be careful* where the colours are applied: if two contrasting colours are mixed the result is mud! For example, paint red over yellow and pink, but not over green. Paint purple over pink, but not over green.

9 Continue adding more stripes in this way until there is a happy balance. As colours are applied over one another, numerous 'new' colours will appear. Leave to dry.

10 Steam and wash, following the instructions given in 'Finishing', page 122.

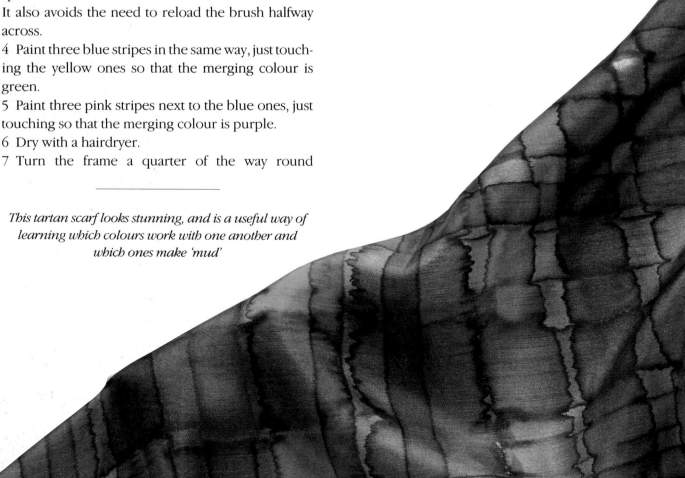

DYE CIRCLES

Creating dye circles is a simple way of experimenting with colour (see 'Techniques' page 17). This simple project reveals more about the behaviour of dyes and shows how they react with one another. As the dyes are applied, watch their reaction. Some – like yellow – disperse the dry colour underneath, sending it away to the edge. Some others mix well, creating new colours.

YOU WILL NEED

masking tape

frame

silk

silk pins

dyes: any colours

palette

dropper

Chinese paintbrush(es)

water pot

paint rag

hairdryer

1 Put masking tape on the frame and stretch on the silk using silk pins, as described on page 14.
2 Transfer dyes to the palette using a dropper or brush (wash clean between each colour).
3 Dip a brush in clean water, remove the excess on a paint rag, load with one of the dyes and, touching the silk with the point of the brush, let the dye form a circle. Allow to dry naturally or dry with a hairdryer. Rinse the brush clean, or use several brushes, one for each colour.
4 Repeat this process with the other colours, creating circles of different colours on the fabric. The cir-

Circles of different coloured dye carefully placed on top of one another create a very interesting effect

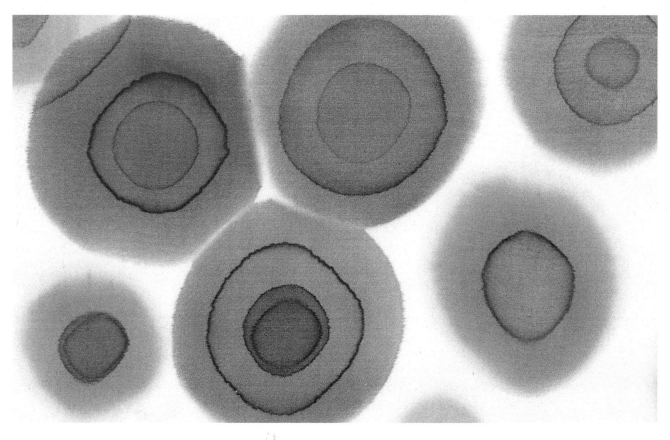

cles should not merge, so keep them well apart from each other. If one looks as if it might 'invade' its neighbours, 'fire' it with a hairdryer.

5 With a clean brush, apply a different colour to the centre of each circle, allowing it to spread and dry.

6 Continue in this way, adding more colours to each circle. Leave to dry.

7 Steam and wash, following the instructions given in 'Finishing', page 122.

ADDITIONS TO THE PAINTBOX

Before starting on the next few projects, increase the contents of the paintbox by adding more colours, a proper palette (if you haven't already got one), a bigger range of brushes, hand-rolled-edge scarves and different salts (rock, flake, dishwasher and table). Keep the salts in screw-top jars away from metal pins.

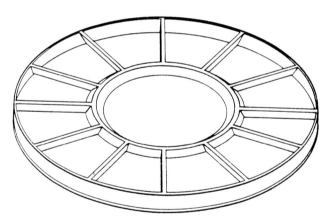

A white plastic artist's palette has compartments for dyes and for mixing colours

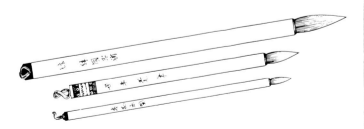

Chinese paintbrushes in several different sizes are ideal for silk painting. The body of the brushes holds a great amount of dye whilst their fine points can reach the smallest area

EASY SALTED STRIPES

As salt attracts water, when it is put on wet paint it produces interesting textured effects. This and the following projects show five different ways salt can be used. Do not throw away all the salt after it has been used; gather some up and store in airtight glass jars, as it can be reused again and again. When these coloured salts are reused some of the dye comes out,

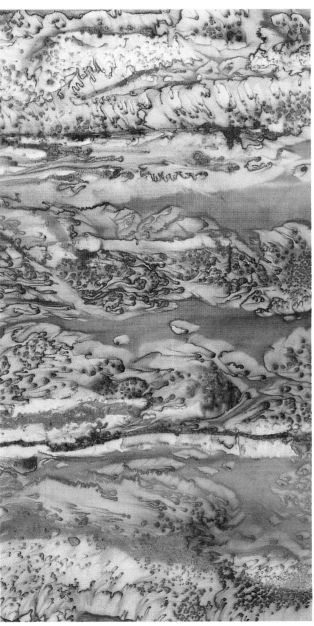

Easy Salted Stripes. *Salt sprinkled over stripes of wet dye gives a wonderful textured result*

giving a slightly textured result, which can add another dimension to a piece of work and is particularly effective for flower centres.

YOU WILL NEED

masking tape

frame

silk

silk pins

dyes: yellow, orange, purple, green, red and grey, or the colours of your choice. (Steam-fixed dyes seem to 'move' better when combined with salt and give more effect than iron-fixed ones. Try both separately.)

palette

dropper

large Chinese paintbrush(es)

water pot

paint rag

salt

1 Put masking tape on the the frame and stretch on the silk using silk pins, as described on page 14.
2 Transfer dyes to the palette using a dropper or brush – wash clean between each colour.
3 Dip a brush in clean water, remove the excess on a paint rag, load with one of the dyes and paint several lines on the silk, leaving strips of white between them. The colour should not be too watery otherwise the salt will not work. Rinse the brush clean, or use several, one for each colour.
4 Repeat this process using other colours which contrast and/or harmonise.
5 Whilst the dyes are still very wet – they need to be wet for the best results – sprinkle the salt over them. As the salt gathers up the dyes it forms textured patterns in the stripes.
6 Leave to dry completely before brushing off the salt.
7 Steam and wash, following the instructions given in 'Finishing', page 122.

SALT AND FLOWERS

YOU WILL NEED

masking tape

frame

55cm (21½in) square silk scarf

silk pins

dyes: pink, blue and yellow (purple, green and orange can be mixed from these)

palette

dropper

Chinese paintbrush(es)

water pot

paint rag

hairdryer

salt

1 Put masking tape on the frame and stretch on the silk using silk pins, as described on page 14.
2 Transfer dyes to the palette using a dropper or brush – wash clean between each colour.
3 Mix together pink and blue to make purple, blue and yellow to make a very pale green, and pink and yellow to make orange.
4 Dip a brush in clean water, remove the excess on a paint rag, load with pink and, using the point of the brush, make several large circles on the silk. Sprinkle a little salt in the centre of each one. Rinse the brush clean, or use several, one for each colour.
5 Repeat this process creating blue and purple circles at random between the pink ones, adding salt *immediately* after they have been painted.
6 Whilst the dyes are still wet, paint areas of soft green between the circles. The wet colours stop spreading when they meet one another.

(*Right*) Salt and Flowers. *Paint silk with circles of colour and sprinkle the centres with salt*

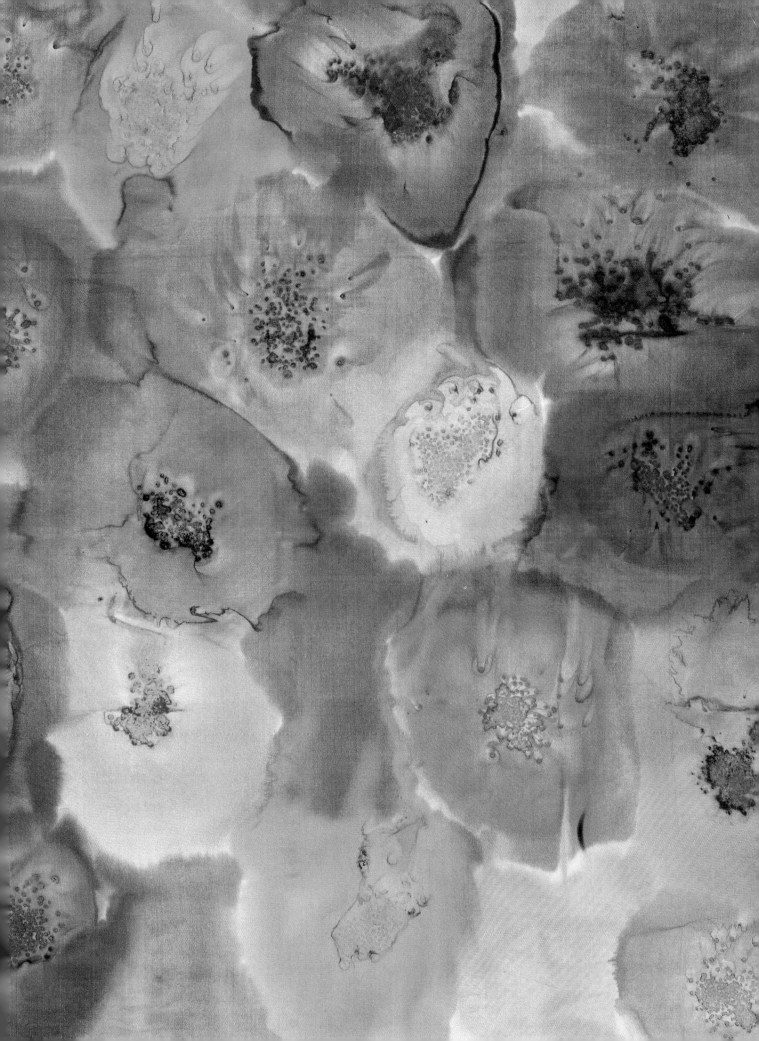

7 Mysterious things happen where the salt is applied. Abstract, three-dimensional flower heads appear, although each one behaves differently, depending on the amount of water and dye used.

8 If the results are disappointing, do not try to alter or rework the design, as this only results in a mess. Brush off the salt, rinse the silk in water, leave to dry and try again. Once salt has been applied, never add more, as this does not work. Only by using salt frequently do you learn how its subtle effects are easily lost by overworking. Once the design is finished, leave it to dry completely before brushing off the salt.

9 Steam and wash, following the instructions given in 'Finishing', page 122.

Salt on the Move. *Allow dye to dribble along the silk then sprinkle with salt*

SALT ON THE MOVE

To achieve these lovely rock-like shapes, tilt the frame slightly before painting, so that the dyes dribble down the silk, and sprinkle on the salt as the dye is moving.

YOU WILL NEED

masking tape

frame

silk

silk pins

dyes: black, grey, emerald, pink, purple and yellow

palette

dropper

large Chinese paintbrushes, one for each colour

salt: rock or dishwasher

1 Put masking tape on the frame and stretch on the silk using the silk pins, as described on page 14.

2 Transfer the dyes to the palette using a dropper or brush – wash clean between each colour.

3 Dip a brush in clean water, remove the excess on a paint rag, load with the first colour and put the point of the brush on the silk at the top of the frame, allowing the colour to dribble down the silk. Sprinkle a little salt over the colour.

4 Repeat this process with the other colours, until the colours merge and the silk is completely covered. Add salt after each colour.

5 Some of the colours may not 'run' the complete length of silk, so just apply more colour at the point they stop. Alternatively, leave the frame tilted at an angle, let the silk dry completely, brush off the salt, turn the frame round 180° so that the bottom becomes the top and start all over again so the colours merge and the silk is covered.

6 Leave the frame tilted at an angle until the silk is completely dry, then brush off the salt.

7 Steam and wash, following the instructions given in 'Finishing', page 122.

CONTROLLING SALT INTO STRIPES

Salt is so invasive that even a tiny speck spoils a smooth background if it is accidentally spilt. To avoid accidents, always paint and completely dry areas that are to be kept smooth before getting out the salt. The crisp stripes in this eye-catching project are defined with gutta and the unsalted stripes are painted first and allowed to dry thoroughly before beginning the salted stripes.

YOU WILL NEED

masking tape

frame

silk

silk pins

pipette of water-based or spirit-based gutta

hairdryer

dyes: turquoise, blue, golden yellow and black

palette

dropper

Chinese paintbrush(es)

water pot

paint rag

salt: coarse or table

1 Put masking tape on the frame and stretch on the silk using silk pins, as described on page 14.
2 Using the gutta, draw stripes across the silk,

Controlling Salt into Stripes. *Highly effective geometric designs can be created with gutta, dye and salt, by sprinkling salt in only some of the painted stripes*

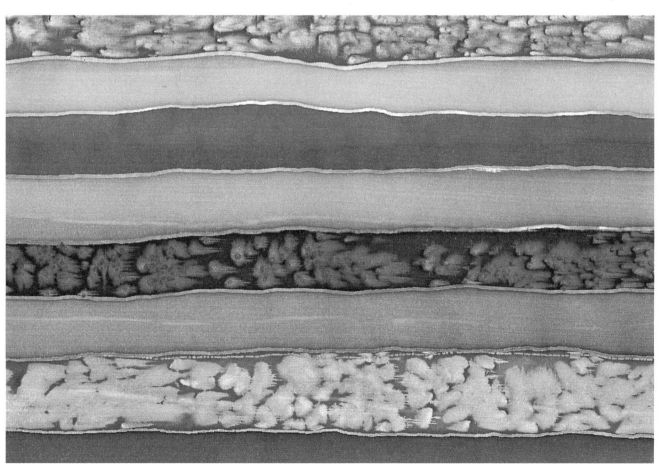

making them roughly the same width apart. Dry with a hairdryer.

3 Transfer dyes to the palette using a dropper or brush – wash clean between each colour.

4 Dip a brush in clean water, remove the excess on a paint rag, load with turquoise and paint some of the stripes. Rinse the brush in clean water, or use several, one for each colour.

5 Repeat this process using blue. Dry with a hairdryer.

6 Paint the remaining stripes yellow, blue, turquoise and black, sprinkling on a little salt as each stripe is painted. The dyes need to be as wet as possible to achieve the best effect. *Be very careful* at this stage. If dry salt falls on dry stripes nothing happens, but if the frame is knocked and *wet salt* is transferred to dry stripes the whole thing may be ruined. Make sure the frame is not in a draught, do not use a hairdryer and try to avoid knocking the frame or the table it is standing on.

7 When the silk is completely dry brush off the salt.

8 Steam and wash, following the instructions given in 'Finishing', page 122.

SOAKING SILK IN SALT

Salt can be used to make a saline solution, which can be painted onto the silk or used to soak it. The silk is then dried with a hairdryer and painted in the normal way. The painted design does not spread as normal, but has an interesting dotted appearance with uneven crystalline edges.

YOU WILL NEED

masking tape
frame
measuring jug
50g (9oz) table salt
spoon for stirring
muslin
large bowl
silk
iron
silk pins
Chinese paintbrush(es)
hairdryer
dyes: any colours
palette
dropper
water pot
paint rag

1 Put masking tape on the frame, as described on page 14.

2 Put 1 litre (1¾pt) warm water in a measuring jug, add the salt and stir until it has dissolved. Leave to stand for one hour.

3 Strain through muslin into a bowl to remove any excess crystals.

4 Put the silk into this saline solution, leave for a few minutes, remove and hang to dry. Lightly iron the dry silk then stretch on the frame using silk pins, as described on page 14.

5 Instead of soaking the silk you could stretch it on the frame first, paint the saline solution over it with a large paintbrush and dry with a hairdryer. Salt rusts metal, so remember to rinse the silk pins in clean water afterwards.

6 Transfer dyes to the palette using a dropper or brush – wash clean between each colour.

7 Load a clean brush with colour and paint the silk with a freehand design, leaving areas of white between the shapes so that the crystal-like edges show up. An attractive texture appears through the painted area as the salt gets to work. Dry with a hairdryer.

8 Steam and wash, following the instructions given in 'Finishing', page 122.

Soaking silk in salt solution prior to painting changes the finished texture of the painted shapes

CHAPTER FIVE

Working with Colour and Gutta

Colour is important to any silk painting, but a bold flowing gutta line can also make a vital contribution to the finished design. All the following examples and projects show how gutta can be used in this positive way.

Artists have their own style and this can be seen in silk painting just as it can in any other form of painting. One particular school uses the white gutta line in a bold positive way so that it is a strong feature of the finished design. Frannie and Katherine Korrell are exponents of this style (see illustrations). The designs (on white silk) feature strong, white gutta lines and bold, bright colours which provide a sharp contrast.

The bold bird and fish design on Katherine Korrell's scarf (overleaf) was drawn with gutta first, before the centre panel was painted blue. Swirls were drawn over the central panel with colourless gutta and then areas of the design were painted a darker shade of blue. No white lines are visible in this area as the gutta was applied onto blue and stayed that colour, allowing the main design to stand out.

To be able to use gutta in this particularly forceful way, the design has to be clear cut, with positive shapes and good strong colours. Because the gutta line makes such an important contribution to the finished effect, it needs to be bold, free and positive. Beginners take note, there is no room for hesitant or shaky lines with such designs.

For some people, a good gutta line is easy to achieve right from the start. For others, strong positive lines come with practice and it can take a while to gain the confidence, correct pressure and even flow required.

It is possible that our personalities are revealed in this medium? On the whole men make very strong gutta lines, so maybe it is the hand strength which governs the results. Whatever the reason, all silk painters will welcome the soft pipettes which are now available and which are much easier to use.

For any design where gutta plays an important role, make sure it is in good condition, that it has a honey-like consistency and flows out of the pipette smoothly and evenly. The relevant merits of water-based and spirit-based guttas have been given on pages 11–12, but at this stage it is worth looking at some of their properties again. Always try to have both types of gutta in the paintbox.

Water-based gutta suits most people, retains a good flowing consistency and does not thicken, although some people say it does not make a good barrier. Certainly it has to be thoroughly dried before any dye is applied, otherwise it will leak.

Spirit-based gutta, on the other hand, is less stable and can be affected by heat. It contains latex and, if left unused in the pipette for a long time in hot conditions, can thicken so much that it does not flow easily. If this happens, pour it into a plastic cup, add some Essence F or white spirit, and mix thoroughly with a spoon. Add a little Essence F at a time until the right consistency is reached. If too much is added the gutta becomes too liquid and the line spreads sideways on the silk.

Strong and positive white gutta lines are a feature of all Frannie's silk fashion accessories

Some water-based metallic guttas do not make good barriers because they are 'one-sided' and sit on the surface of the silk – the metallic powders which they are made from do not penetrate fabric. Always try them out first, as different brands vary a great deal. Sometimes it is better to use them for surface decoration only, rather than for barrier lines (or paint on both sides of the silk).

From a personal point of view, it would be helpful if manufacturers could put the expected lifespan of their guttas on the tubes, indicating their 'use by' date. Also, it would be useful to know the colour fastness of all the dyes as some seem to be very short-lived. One way would be to show colour reliability on a one-to-nine scale, enabling users to avoid those with short-lived colour fastness and choose the right dyes for a particular work.

The following four projects demonstrate how gutta can be used in the positive way described at the beginning of this chapter, although not necessarily using strong white outlines.

A strong white gutta line can be an integral part of a design as seen in this lovely scarf by Katherine Korrell

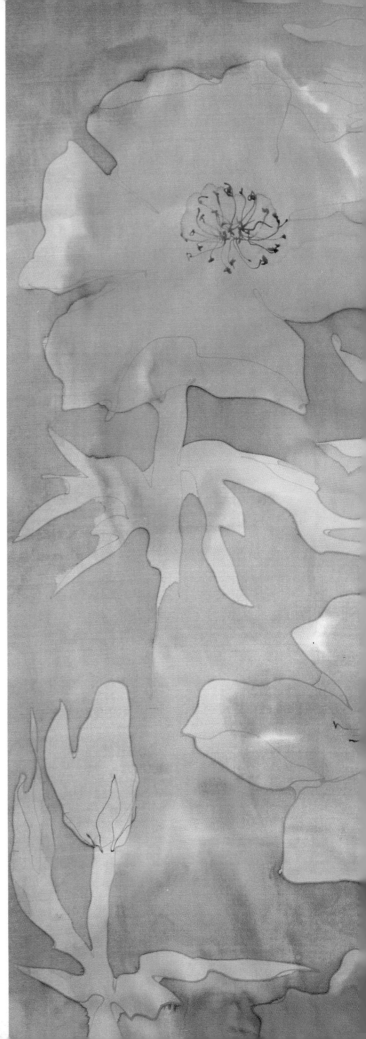

FREEHAND FLOWERS

These freehand flowers show a bold and uninhibited, yet balanced, application of colour. This is the result of colouring all the silk, then applying gutta. Having learnt the marvellous feeling of dribbling dye and salt on silk in the previous chapter, combine this new-found freedom with some controlled gutta work.

YOU WILL NEED

masking tape

large frame

silk

silk pins

dyes: purple, pink, camellia (soft red), blue, yellow and turquoise

palette

dropper

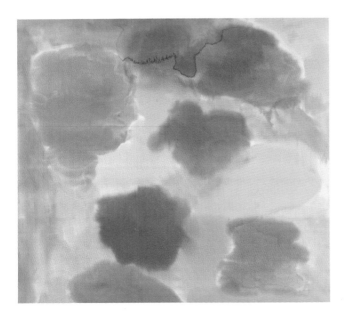

Freehand Flowers (*right*) *shows how a gutta design can be applied after the colour. The photograph above shows the coloured areas before the gutta is applied*

large Chinese paintbrushes

paint rag

water pot

hairdryer

pipette of colourless gutta

pipette of black or metallic-grey gutta

1 Put masking tape on the frame and stretch on the silk using silk pins, as described on page 14.

2 Transfer dyes to the palette, using a dropper for each colour.

3 Dip a brush in clean water, remove the excess on a paint rag, load with purple and paint the purple areas as shown.

4 Follow with the pink, camellia, blue, yellow and turquoise areas. Paint these areas of colour quickly and freely.

5 On the palette, mix blue and yellow to make a soft green and use it to paint any remaining white areas. Create a few grey areas by painting over some of the soft green with purple. When it is finished no white silk should be visible. This technique illustrates how wet colours stop and do not merge when they meet each other. Dry with a hairdryer.

6 Using the pipette of colourless gutta, draw freehand flower, leaf and stem shapes over the silk, letting the gutta drawing spill over the colours in a free uninhibited way.

7 Using the pipette of black or metallic grey gutta, draw in the flower centres.

8 When the gutta is dry, paint more colour round the outside or on the inside of the flower shapes so that they stand out from the background. The brush needs to be well loaded with watery dye so the result remains soft and delicate. Don't always wash out the brush between applying colours. Colours left to mix on the brush often result in beautiful, subtle tones which are impossible to mix. Avoid putting together shades of green and red, as only muddy colours will appear. Purple over green makes a pleasant grey. Leave to dry.

9 Steam and wash, following the instructions given in 'Finishing', page 122.

THE PARROT TULIP

The parrot tulip makes a striking subject. As with Freehand Flowers, the silk is covered completely with paint, so that the gutta lines do not show up white. Once the gutta design is drawn, more colour is applied. This wet-on-dry technique adds another dimension to the design, particularly around the tulip centre.

YOU WILL NEED

masking tape

frame

silk

silk pins

embroiderer's pen

dyes: canary yellow, red, blue and pink

palette

dropper

Chinese paintbrushes

water pot

paint rag

hairdryer

pipette of colourless gutta

pipette of black gutta

1 Put masking tape on the frame and stretch on the silk using silk pins, as described on page 14.

2 Dip a brush in clean water, remove the excess on a paint rag, load with canary yellow and apply *freely* over the silk where the tulip head, stem and leaves are to be drawn. Dry with a hairdryer.

3 If tracing the tulip design from the original shown here, transfer it onto the yellow silk with an em-

The Parrot Tulip shows how white gutta lines can be avoided by painting the silk with colour before the design is drawn

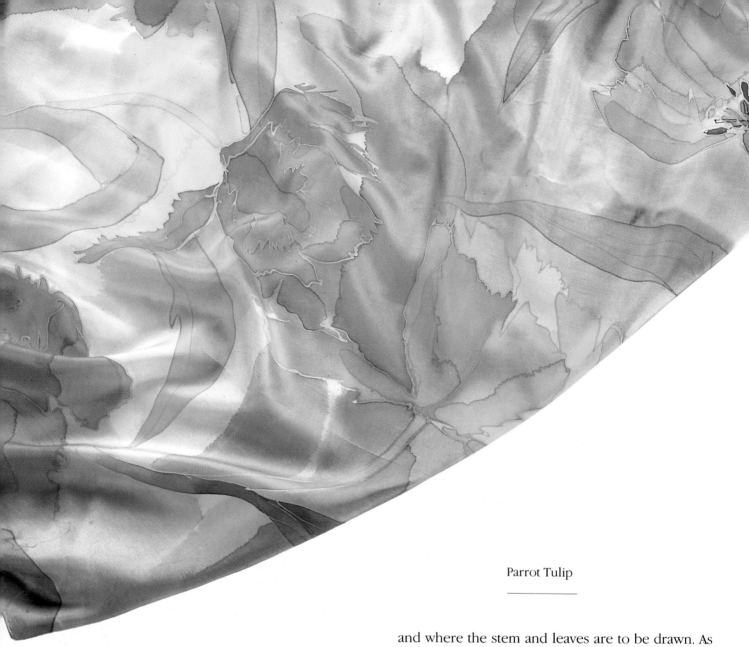

Parrot Tulip

broiderer's pen, using one of the methods described on page 26.

4 Transfer dyes to the palette using a dropper or brush – wash clean between each colour.

5 Using the colourless gutta, draw on the petals, making sure each one is completely outlined finishing at the centre. These lines remain yellow after the silk has been steamed and washed.

6 On the palette, use canary yellow and red to mix different shades of orange, then use these colours to paint over the yellow tulip head to create an interesting shaded effect. Because yellow, orange and red all belong to the same colour family they harmonise well.

7 Using blue, paint the area around the tulip head and where the stem and leaves are to be drawn. As blue is painted over yellow, green is produced.

8 Using the colourless gutta, draw on the stem and leaves. Dry with a hairdryer or leave to dry.

9 On the palette, mix pink and blue to make purple, and paint behind the stem and leaves. The grey/green and purple result will provide a contrast to the stems and leaves.

10 Hot red and orange against a totally blue-green background are too much of a contrast and need tying together. Add red to part of the background and a purple shadow to one side of the tulip to add depth. This also gives a better balance and provides a richness and warmth to echo the flower.

11 Using the black gutta, paint the stamens. Leave to dry.

12 Steam and wash, following the instructions given in 'Finishing', page 122.

PANSY SCARF

Pansy shapes and colours lend themselves to a variety of treatments. Here, the design is very free, with a riot of flowers seemingly scattered over the surface. This pansy scarf is a very liberating project and great fun, as the shapes are developed as the work progresses.

YOU WILL NEED

tracing paper or newspaper

soft pencil

scissors

masking tape

frame to fit silk

90cm (35in) square silk scarf

silk pins

embroiderer's pen

pipette of colourless gutta

dyes: turquoise, blue, violet, yellow and orange

palette

dropper

Chinese paintbrushes

water pot

diluant

paint rag

hairdryer

metallic-grey gutta

gold and silver gutta

Pansy Scarf is a riot of scattered pansies in a much freer design than in Pot of Pansies (page 62)

1 On tracing paper or newspaper use a soft pencil to draw about ten, large pansy shapes. Cut out with scissors.

2 Put masking tape on the frame and stretch on the silk using silk pins, as described on page 14.

3 A stretched metre of white silk may appear daunting at first, but breaking up the area by scattering over cut-out pansy shapes is a good way to start. The aim of this project is to cover the background with colour, leaving the white pansies to stand out.

4 Take the cut-out shapes and place them over the silk, moving them around until you get a balance. These areas remain white.

5 Using an embroiderer's pen, draw round the shapes.

6 Using the colourless gutta, outline the pansies, carefully following the petal lines to the centres and drawing in the flower centres.

7 Transfer turquoise, blue, violet and yellow dyes to the palette with a dropper or brush – wash clean between each colour. On the palette, mix the turquoise, blue and violet separately with diluant.

8 Dip a medium-sized brush in clean water, remove the excess on a paint rag, load with turquoise and paint the background around one flower.

9 Dip the unwashed brush in a little water, add some yellow to produce a soft green and use to cover more of the background. Rinse the brush clean.

10 Load the brush with violet and paint next to the other colours so they merge.

11 Gradually cover the background in this way, balancing the colours where possible. Add blue and more green until all the background is painted, leaving the white flowers untouched.

12 Generally it is not a good idea to work with an unwashed brush, but when working on a free design like this it does add to the results. Just add a little water to the 'dirty' brush at times to give soft shades and mysterious mixtures of the background colours which add to the effect. Dry with a hairdryer or leave to dry naturally.

13 Using the colourless gutta, draw more pansy shapes freehand on the background, adding leaves and stems. Leave to dry.

14 Load a brush with violet, and paint inside a few of the outlined flowers. Repeat using blue on some of the other flowers. Alternatively, add more colour to the background around the new flowers to make them stand out, as described in 'Freehand Flowers', page 56. As more colour is applied, wet or dry lines appear, adding to the effect and becoming part of the design.

Pansy Scarf with Scattered Pansies, the latter showing separate pansy shapes scattered against a smooth alcohol-mixed background, with a bold use of black and white gutta

15 Paint in some flower petals without a gutta outline, using a hairdryer to stop the colours spreading
too far. This can be very effective as the petals form
lovely soft impressions of pansies (see detail). Leave
to dry.

16 Add more leaves and flower details. Use metallic-

grey gutta for drawing the 'faces' of the pansies and gold and silver gutta to outline some of the leaves and petals and for adding details. Metallic guttas only show on one side of the silk, so use them on both sides of the scarf.

17 Steam and wash, following the instructions given in 'Finishing', page 122.

POT OF PANSIES

With their irregular petals and very positive bright-orange or yellow centres, pansies are particularly interesting to paint. To familiarise yourself with their shape, draw the flowers in a sketch book from all angles before drawing them on the silk (a useful habit whatever the subject matter). This fairly structured design is ideal for beginners

YOU WILL NEED

masking tape

frame

silk about 45 x 35cm (18 x 14in)

silk pins

embroiderer's pen

pipette of colourless gutta

coloured guttas: blue, purple, green and metallic grey

hairdryer

dyes: grey, turquoise, violet, blue and yellow

palette

dropper

two or three Chinese paintbrushes of various sizes

water pot

paint rag

diluant

1 Put masking tape on the frame and stretch on the silk using silk pins, as described on page 14.

2 Using an embroiderer's pen, draw the pot of pan-sies freehand on the silk, adding an horizon line behind to show the table edge, and putting stripes on the cloth to give perspective.

3 Using the colourless gutta, outline the white pansies and glass vase. Using the blue and purple gutta, outline the coloured pansies. Using the green gutta, outline the leaves.

4 Transfer dyes to the palette using a dropper or brush – wash clean between each colour.

5 Dip a brush in clean water, remove the excess on a paint rag, load with grey and paint the grey shadow on the table top next to the vase.

6 Using the colourless, green and metallic-grey guttas, draw the pansy lying on the table and the lines of the cloth. Dry with a hairdryer.

7 Paint the pansies and leaves the appropriate colours.

8 Once the subject matter has been painted, decide on a background colour. Touches of the violet chosen are present in the flowers so this is ideal. Mix violet dye with diluant, not water, to ensure a smooth, even result. Mix enough to cover the whole area in one go so there are no watermarks – this happens if the work has to be left whilst you mix more – and to ensure a consistent colour as it is often impossible to make exactly the same colour again. (It is personal choice whether the background is painted first or last, but to me it seems better to choose the background and foreground colours after the main subject matter of the design has been painted.)

9 Paint the stripes on the cloth, picking out the colours of the flowers and the background to give co-ordination.

10 Shade the white flowers with a little grey.

11 Paint in the yellow flower centres. Draw in some of the pansy faces with metallic-grey gutta to give more definition. Leave to dry.

12 Steam, iron and wash, following the instructions given in 'Finishing', page 122. Remember to iron *before* washing to fix the metallic guttas.

Pot of Pansies *was drawn using coloured and colourless gutta*

CHAPTER SIX

Sources of Design

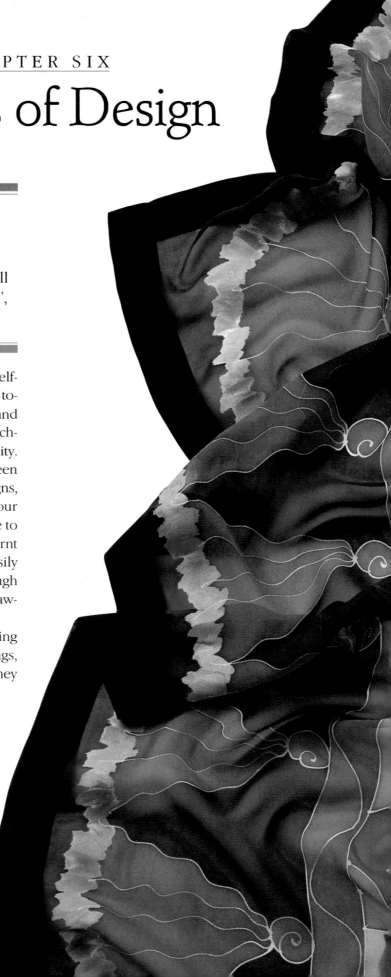

Designing worries a lot of people, even though it simply means placing shapes and colour together in an interesting and pleasing way. And the sources of design are all around us – the secret is learning how to 'see', which means developing an artistic eye.

Silk painting is a wonderful vehicle for self-expression. At first it is a way of putting together colours, finding out how they mix and the effects they create. Learning these techniques is great fun and requires little drawing ability.

Once all possible colour combinations have been explored by painting patterns and abstract designs, the next step is to learn how to control colour through drawing. There is no magic to being able to draw and it is not something which can only be learnt at an art school, in fact the technicalities can be easily learnt at evening classes and developed through drawing practice, especially still lifes and life drawing. The real secret is learning how to 'see'.

Learn to 'see' and you are well on the way to being able to draw. When artists look at their surroundings, they see shapes, colours and patterns, which they often store in their sketchbooks for later use.

Tassels by Joy Butler, a wonderful amalgamation of different designs

FEATHERS

Try to develop your artistic expression with this project, which is a simple way of creating a design by placing shapes together. Just remember that design is a way of placing shapes and colours together in an interesting way until a pleasing arrangement and harmony is created. Get rid of any inhibitions, awaken the artist in you and start stimulating your imagination. Everyday objects, like these feathers, have a structure and beauty which is often ignored. Once recognised, they can become the basis of many different designs.

This small feather drawing, found in a magazine, was enlarged to several different sizes on a photocopier and copied onto both white paper and clear acetate – this can be done at art shops and on certain photocopiers. Cut out the shapes and place them on a card, moving them around to create an interesting and pleasing arrangement, this can be done more easily with clear acetate. Once you are satisfied with the design, look at the way the lines relate to one another, look at the patches of light and dark and the areas of white showing between each outline. Could they be copied or adapted in some way for a silk painting, could part of the design be used in a creative way? This is all part of the process of designing.

The same treatment can be applied to leaves, particularly transparent autumn leaves which only have gossamer-like veins, or any small interesting drawing. First create a design, then study it to see how it can be used.

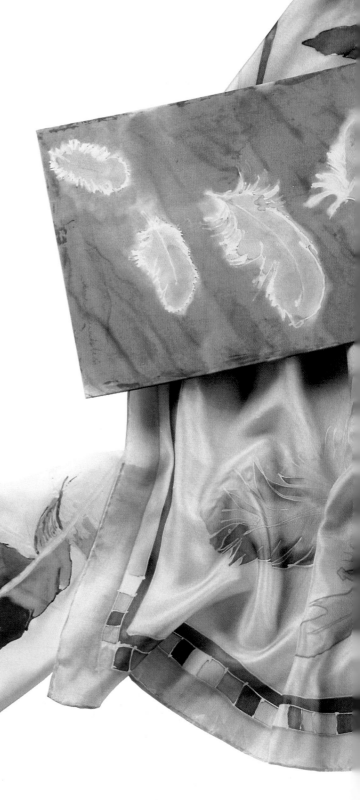

Placing simple shapes – like this photocopied feather – into an interesting and pleasing arrangement is a good way of creating an attractive design

THE CREATIVE BRAIN

For some people, creating designs presents no problem at all, whereas others really have to work at it. The reason why some people seem naturally creative and others are not, lies in the way the brain works.

The right-hand side of the brain is the creative side, the left-hand side is the sensible, practical, thinking part. Because the left side dominates the right, and often gets overwhelmed by the sheer practicalities of everyday life, the right side may not get the chance to develop fully – if at all. Having a job, looking after a family, running a home, worrying about the family budget, etc, means the left-hand side of the brain is active most of the time, preventing the right-hand side from getting the time and peace it needs to develop.

Creative people tend to be those who have been allowed, found or made the time – at art school for example – to develop the right side of their brains. If it is fully developed, this side may even take control so that when such a person is painting, writing or doing anything 'creative' other thoughts seem to disappear. The tell-tale signs of a creative person are easy to spot. Such people tend to lack organisational skills, they do not listen with attention when someone is talking to them, seeming pre-occupied, they forget the passage of time, so may miss meals, burn cakes, forget luncheon appointments, even forget to eat! When the right side of the brain is in action the left side does not get a look in.

However, I know from my own experience that it is possible to 'switch off' the practical side of life and allow the creative side to take over. This does, of course need practice, and time.

Designing is a matter of selection and rejection all the time, which can be totally exhausting. Even people whose creative side has been developed need time and peace to work. Time and peace are essential ingredients for creativity, and finding them with today's busy lifestyles is not always easy. Even if you find the time it is not always easy to 'switch on': you have to be in the right frame of mind to work.

Sometimes getting up early in the morning gives golden moments of peace and quiet with no interruptions. At other times inspiration strikes suddenly and the only way to develop it is to lock yourself

away. There may be times when, despite the peace and quiet, something is not working out, when you have a mental block. Don't worry, put the work to one side, so it can be seen as you work on other things or where you will see it as you wake the next day. If the work is left for a while, when you come back to it the solution can often be found.

IN SEARCH OF DESIGN

Just like learning how to 'see', so you can learn how to design, using one of the following methods of observation.

The most exciting way of creating a design is through first-hand observation, by seeing something which fires your imagination and makes you stop to take a second look. It could be the way light falls on an object, the pattern on an airport floor, a manhole cover, textured wall, cracked ice, a particular mixture of colours and flowers – anything. Because inspiration can strike at any time, many artists carry a sketchbook to 'capture' the idea at the time and develop it further at home.

Then there is second-hand observation, when inspiration comes from seeing someone else's work, the work of an artist or sculptor in a gallery, in books or on postcards, or by seeing shapes and patterns in photographs, pictures and magazines. This can happen, even subconsciously, to the extent that you may even change your style and method of working. An Andy Warhol work influenced my picture *Wild Silk*. He used colour freely on the paper and then added drawing over it, a technique which I found very inspiring.

Way to the Sea was influenced by a postcard of a sandy path to the sea by Winifred Nicholson, which was sent to me shortly before I went on holiday to Cornwall. It was hot that year, the sea was particularly still, the sky shimmered, the heatwave stayed and my *Way to the Sea* was sketched in pencil in the dunes under a parasol, and later painted in the shade. It is a reminder of that hot, sunny day, and shows how influence can act subconsciously.

Wild Silk (inspired by an Andy Warhol painting) shows a new freedom of colour

Way to the Sea

DIVERSITY OF DESIGN

Designs can be inspired by anything and everything around us, but to me travel is particularly creative. Visiting different places and experiencing different sights and sensations result in a whole host of images to be captured, either in a sketchbook or by photographs, and translated into a design at a later date. Whether it is the sea, flowers, fish or just the sky, they are real, you can see them, even touch and smell them, observe the delicacy of their colours and the details of their structure.

A shell will inspire some people but not others, as will certain scenes, a flower, a bird or texture. Your eyes reflect what *you* are looking at and this image is very individual. A group of people all using the same subject matter for their design will produce many interesting and highly different results, which is fascinating to see.

Diversity of design can be seen with these fish

John Farmelo's fish have a charming simplicity, accentuated by quilting and machine embroidery

examples. Fish are interesting subjects to paint, they shimmer and gleam enticingly and have interesting yet strong shapes. Black and grey gutta were used to draw *Mackerels* (opposite) and, although the fish had plenty of colour, the problem was capturing the shimmer. Mother-of-pearl Deka fabric paint mixed

with lilac, turquoise and yellow, provided the solution. Applied in blobs, it shimmered and gave an exciting three-dimensional impression to the fish. Silver gutta could be used if Deka is not available.

Mackerels is very different from the other two examples shown. When imagination is allowed full uninhibited rein, wonderful things can happen and imaginary shapes and colours emerge. John Farmelo's fish have a simplicity about them, making a lovely subject for a cushion. By masking the fish with

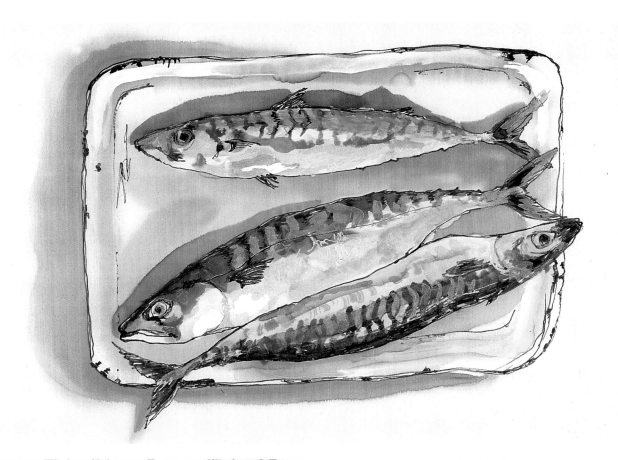

Mackerel

paper shapes, the background was sprayed with dye, then the fish were painted in shades of blue. The technique of spraying is done using a simple mouth-blown diffuser which is cheap and readily available from craft shops. The white outline was accentuated with quilting and machine embroidery, which was also used around the outside edge.

SEQUENCES

This sequence of artichoke paintings shows how an idea can develop from a single subject. The first painting was the result of seeing some artichokes with their lovely shapes on sale in a French market. Although I always carry a frame, some silk and a few

*The simplest of fish designs, on a South American
block-printed paper*

dyes with me on holiday 'just in case', the range of available colours was limited so a certain amount of experimentation was necessary. The single artichoke was sketched on the silk with a waterproof Edding pen as an embroiderer's pen was not available. (The Edding pen can be used on silk without bleeding sidewards, so is a very useful addition to the paintbox.) Green gutta was used to draw over the pen outline, then grey, yellow, turquoise and blue dyes were added. Colourless gutta was applied over the top and more colour added to finish it.

Painting number two was done the following day, as the artichokes lay on a plate. The shadows were important to the overall design as was the shape of the plate.

These three paintings show how ideas can develop from a single subject. First came the single artichoke, then the artichokes on a plate. Finally the shape was abstracted to create this interesting scarf design (right)

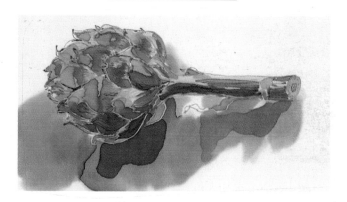

Returning home to England I noticed some artichoke leaves in the garden; they made me look at artichokes in a totally different way Now I had their shape in my mind I could abstract it and use colour to create a totally different design. The result was the artichoke scarf, created with only four colours – purple, turquoise, blue and green. Pale grey was created by mixing purple and green.

First, the artichoke shapes were arranged in an interesting way on the silk and drawn on with green gutta. At first, the effect was rather dull, then the leaves – being such lovely shapes – were used to break up the background, creating interesting shapes between shapes, right up to the edge. A border was drawn, broken up by the leaves and painted a rich purple. Finally silver gutta was added in the shape of extra leaves.

A STATE OF GRACE

Inspiration does not always come easily and if you see something which excites you, you may not be able to capture it in the way you would like. Do not worry, you cannot always work in an inspired way so do not expect it. Nevertheless when it does happen, a feeling of well-being seems to appear, the work flows along and can leave you feeling exhausted yet happy The flow of adrenalin can be felt when a painting seems to be developing as you want it to. It is a feeling which is very difficult to put into words and may not happen very often, but you feel exhilarated that the work has progressed and is good, my expression for it is a 'state of grace'.

SCRAPBOOK OF IDEAS

Keeping your own scrapbook of ideas is one way of building up a readily available source of design. Just stick in all the pictures that capture your imagination, irrespective of what it is that appeals. It could be the shapes or colours of flowers, stones, leaves, anything, even the relationship of light and dark caused by shadows. Add photographs of scenes and items you like. Stick in pieces of interesting fabric, or simply strips of colours that you find exciting. Make it your scrapbook of anything and everything that pleases *you*. Cut out pictures from magazines, stick in postcards, feathers and leaves. Looking through such a

scrapbook often releases a trigger in your mind, and it can be the source of an idea which develops into a whole sequence of designs like my artichokes.

London, New York, Sydney, Paris and many other cities throughout the world are well served with superb sources of design in their galleries and museums. You will be amazed how an idea can be triggered off by a visit to a museum; ammonite shapes once gave me the source for a quilted cushion. See what inspires *you*. Take a sketchbook with

you and visit your local museum or gallery, and do not be embarrassed to stand and draw an exciting motif, an ancient pot or unusual statue.

Do not forget either that in everyday life you are surrounded by sources of inspiration – scattered sweets, a group of cabbages at the greengrocers or in your garden, wrought iron work – the list is endless so take the time to look around you.

Compile your own scrapbook of ideas using everything and anything that appeals to you

CHAPTER SEVEN

The Natural World

The natural world is a wonderful and endless source of inspiration. Many of the scenes found by the sea and in the country make perfect subjects for silk painting, from shells, fish and lobsters, to birds, butterflies and flowers.

Although the natural world is full of exciting subjects, silk painting 'on location' is not to be recommended for the beginner. Initially it is much better to capture the details in a sketchbook, drawing a rough outline and jotting down details of the colours, then return home to paint it. As your confidence grows and you become more adept with gutta and paintbrush, put together a travelling paintbox so that you always have the essentials if you are suddenly inspired.

Sea and Sand, *showing the seashore on a calm, sunny day*

TRAVELLING PAINTBOX

All the equipment in a travelling paintbox should be as light as possible. Carrying a made-up frame can be rather cumbersome, so buy some wooden oil canvas stretchers of different lengths – available from good art shops – with the corners mitred and grooved as shown (right) so they are interchangeable and will make up frames of various sizes as required.

To carry around all the equipment, some form of carrying case or artbin is required. Artbins are ideal and can be bought at art shops, although cheaper versions – intended for carrying tools, etc – can be bought at hardware stores.

EQUIPMENT AND MATERIALS

frames(s) of various sizes made from:
    two x 30cm (12in) lengths oil canvas stretchers
    two x 15cm (6in) lengths oil canvas stretchers
    two x 20cm (8in) lengths oil canvas stretchers

palette (unwieldy but essential)

artbin containing:
    silk pins
    water-based gutta in a pipette
    black and grey gutta bought made-up
    two Chinese paintbrushes
    cotton wool buds
    scissors
    silk
    masking tape
    tiny pot of white
    fabric paint
    empty pipettes
    and nibs
    spare gutta
    Edding pen 0.3 nib
    sketchbook and pencil
    dyes: two yellows,
    hot pink, emerald, blue,
    red and grey-black

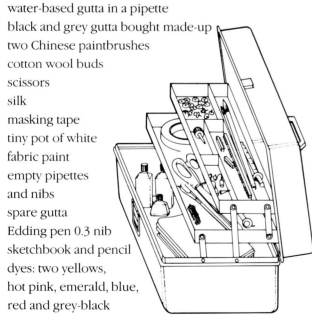

The most important part of any travelling paintbox is the artbin, which should hold all the equipment – except the palette and frame

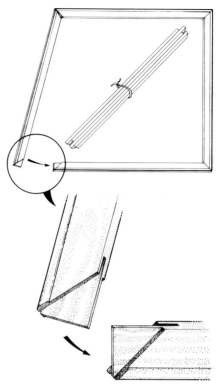

Make a travelling frame from lengths of oil canvas stretchers, mitred in the corners so they are interchangeable, which slot together when required

THEMES FROM THE SEA: SEA AND SAND

The mood of the sea is constantly changing and the colours of the sky and sea on a clear calm day are very different to those in bad weather, so a seascape makes a challenging subject to paint. Despite its changing mood, nothing is more elusive than a wave; it moves, it changes, it rolls, it leaves foam, and a moment of movement is hard to capture. Study an 'angry' sea and very little pure white is present, although tones of white and green can be seen and dark shadows appear under the foam.

Using just a few colours, this simple painting (opposite) captures the atmosphere of a summer's day, recalling the heat of the day and the sound of the sea. Several techniques have been used, including wet-on-wet for the background, wet-on-dry for the detail in the sky and sea, and salt for the beach. The horizon needs to be drawn freely and not with a ruler – the horizon never appears straight to the naked eye.

YOU WILL NEED

masking tape
frame
silk
silk pins
dyes: blue, emerald, warm yellow, brown and grey
palette
dropper
Chinese paintbrush
water pot
pipette of colourless gutta
salt

1 Put masking tape on the frame and stretch on the silk using silk pins, as described on page 14.

2 Transfer dyes to the palette using droppers or brushes.

3 On the palette, mix together blue and emerald to make turquoise.

4 Dip a brush in clean water, load with pale blue and use to completely cover the top two-thirds of the silk for the sky and sea, then add streaks for water and deeper shades of blue to create the contrasts. Leave the bottom third free of colour for the beach. Rinse the brush clean.

5 Load brush with a mix of brown and yellow and paint the foreground a warm sandy colour to create the beach.

6 When dry, using the pipette of gutta, draw on the horizon freehand. Leave to dry.

7 Load the brush with turquoise and add this colour to the sky above the horizon.

8 Add some deep blue below the gutta line to show the distant horizon. Using turquoise and blue, add wave effects close to the beach. This wet-on-dry technique makes delicate and attractive watermarks.

9 Using the pipette of gutta, draw in some rock outlines on the beach. Leave to dry.

10 On the palette, mix together brown and yellow to make a sand colour. Load the brush and paint the rocks and foreground of the beach, sprinkle on salt sparingly and leave to dry. The salt draws up the colours to resemble a sandy beach. When completely dry, brush off the salt.

11 Using a clean brush loaded with pale blue, dab over the yellow rocks to give the impression of green seaweed.

12 If any of the colours seem too bright, paint over with a wash of diluted grey to tone them down.

13 Steam and wash, following the instructions given in 'Finishing', page 122. If you are unable to steam and wash when on holiday, keep the silk out of sunlight until you return home. The colours will not fade in that short time, but keep the work away from water as it is not yet fixed.

WILD SEA

In bad weather, the sky and sea look very different. The colours are deeper, with the sky colours bruised, and the waves of a stormy sea contain very little white. Creating flecks of sharp white on silk can be a problem. One solution is to use Deka permanent white fabric paint. No doubt painting waves could be tackled in other ways, so study them and develop your own techniques to capture that transient moment of movement.

Deka permanent paint, which comes in silver, pearl and gold as well as white and other colours, is water soluble and mixes with most types of dye, yet it remains opaque (as in *Mackerels*, page 71). Because it contains a thickener, it does not spread on silk but sits on top of the other colours like gouache. Colourfast after ironing, it can be steamed and washed with steam-fixed dyes, making it a useful addition to the paintbox.

YOU WILL NEED

masking tape
frame
silk
silk pins
dyes: purple, dark green, blue and yellow
palette

dropper

Chinese paintbrushes

water pot

paint rag

pipette of colourless gutta

Deka permanent white fabric paint

1 Put masking tape on the frame and stretch on the silk using silk pins, as described on page 14.
2 Transfer dyes to the palette using droppers or brushes.
3 On the palette, mix some purple and green to make a pale grey.
4 Dip a brush in clean water, load with blue and start painting from the top downwards. Add some grey

Wild Sea depicts the seashore on a grey, windy day

and continue. Add purple to the brush when painting over the horizon area. Add some green for the sea. This wet-on-wet technique creates a lovely watery effect of mixed colour as the dyes merge into one another.
5 Create pale shades of green and blue/green by adding water. Use them to paint the centre third of the silk for the sea. Rinse the brush clean.
6 Load brush with diluted yellow and paint the bottom third of the silk yellow for the sand, meeting in a soft watery join at the sea edge.
7 Apply a strip of pale yellow to the sea just below the horizon line to appear as sand. Leave to dry.
8 Using the gutta, draw the horizon line freehand. Leave to dry.

9 To create a turbulent-looking sea, add touches of purple and green in front of the horizon line. Leave to dry.

10 Only the very peaks of the waves reflect pure white. Put some Deka permanent white on the palette, mix with a little green, and paint the crests of the waves.

11 Before the paint is dry, paint in the shadows under the waves using a dark green. They will blend at the edges and appear soft. Leave to dry.

12 Add flecks of pure white to the very peaks of the waves. Rinse the brush.

13 Load brush with a pale watery green and add a watery reflection on the beach. Leave to dry.

14 Steam and wash, following the instructions given in 'Finishing', page 122. Fix according to the dyes used, remembering to iron *after* steaming and *before* washing if you have used steam-fixed dyes with the iron-fixed Deka fabric paint.

SEASHORE SCARF

Sitting at the edge of the sea, letting it lap round your feet, you will notice the various shapes and colours formed by the foam, always very elusive and always changing. This scarf design captures the moment after the sea has broken on the shore and is just running back, forming an edge of foam. Gutta is used to outline the edge of the foam and the different areas of colour on the sand. A few mussel shells have been included among the pebbles to give additional interest. The design divides the scarf in half diagonally; one half is turquoise/blue, the other sandy yellow.

Although this is an ambitious project, it is well worth trying. Or, just read through it and the technique may inspire you to create your own seashore designs (see Other Seashore Ideas, page 83).

YOU WILL NEED

masking tape

frame

silk scarf square

silk pins

pipette of colourless gutta

embroiderer's pen

steam-fixed dyes: blue, turquoise, canary yellow, brown, hot pink and black

palette

dropper

Chinese paintbrush

water pot

paint rag

black and silver gutta

1 Put masking tape on the frame and stretch on the silk using silk pins, as described on page 14.

2 Because of the importance of the white foam, use a pipette of colourless gutta to draw a lapping line diagonally across the scarf. Add more lines and outlines for the foam shapes. Use an embroiderer's pen to mark the foam areas to be left white with a 'W'. Leave to dry.

3 Transfer dyes to the palette with droppers or brushes.

4 Dip a brush in clean water, load with blue and turquoise and paint the areas between the white foam on the sea half. Leave the areas marked 'W' free of colour.

5 On the beach side, use black and colourless gutta to draw the shell and pebble outlines, including the barnacles found on the shells.

6 Load the brush with pale yellow and paint the beach. Leave to dry.

7 Keeping the very corner of the beach area pale yellow, paint over the rest of the beach with a deeper shade of brown/yellow, to give the impression of the shades on the sand caused by receding water.

8 Whilst the yellow is still wet, paint the shore area along the white foam line with a slightly deeper brown/yellow. Over this area, scatter some salt sparingly to create a wet sand appearance. Leave to dry. Brush off the salt.

9 On the palette, mix together some hot pink and a little blue to make mauve; mix this with some silver

This Seashore Scarf *is a picture of contrasts*

gutta and a little black dye to create a pearlised colour and use to paint the mussel shells. Using grey and black gutta, draw curved lines on the shells to make them appear more realistic.

10 Paint the pebbles a very watery mauve and pale blue.

11 Add more blue to the sea, creating swirls and eddies until a reasonable balance is achieved. Aim for a feeling of movement to contrast with the still, hot sand.

12 Steam and wash, as described in 'Finishing', page 122. The colours of the finished work should glow with a sheen and vibrancy, reflecting the contrast between the sizzling sand and the cool sea with its refreshing, lapping waves.

*(Above) Individual interpretation of a subject is
important. Compare this realistic lobster painting with
the vivid panel (below) by Katherine Korrell, with its bold
gutta lines and exciting colours*

OTHER SEASHORE IDEAS

There are plenty of other inspiring subjects by the sea. Shells and pebbles have an unusual lustre which makes them glimmer and gleam at the water's edge. Fish and lobsters have fascinating and sometimes complex shapes, whether the finished result is abstract or realistic. The following examples show a selection of different approaches.

Under the Ocean

An abstract approach to a subject can look stunning, as illustrated by the sea-inspired panel by Katherine Korrell. Katherine, an experienced silk painter who studied at art school, drew the design freehand and it developed as she worked on the fabric. The stylised shapes of fish, starfish and lobster and the divided background were drawn using bold gutta lines, then painted in brilliant colours. This is a particularly clever device which adds to the excitement of the work.

Look at the way the background has been painted. It may appear simple but great care has been taken to choose the right colours to set off the different coloured fish: yellow behind blue, blue behind red,

yellow behind pink. The combinations provide a lovely balance and give the design great energy.

Lobsters

Compared to Katherine Korrell's sea scene, the lobsters (left) show a totally different, more realistic, style of silk painting, although the subject matter is very similar.

The two lobsters have been drawn using a much more conventional still life approach with few colours. Like Katherine's vibrant panel, the background is very important to the finished design, although in this design a black and white tablecloth provides the foil for the stark white dish and red lobsters. The old cracked bread-bin lid and two lobsters were captured using red and black gutta. The texture of the shells was created with salt.

Shells

Mussel shells are lovely subjects to paint. Look at one from all angles and follow its lines as they flow round and round. Try to draw these flowing lines on paper before attempting to do so on silk. It may be easier to create the shapes with black gutta instead of a pencil

or pen, as gutta lines flow more naturally.

In the example shown the shell outlines were drawn with metallic-grey and black gutta. Silver water-based gutta was mixed on the palette with mauve and blue dyes and these colours were used to paint the shells. The combination captures the natural colour and gives off that delicate sheen found in mussel shells. Small areas of navy and purple were added and small stars of silver gutta applied to form the barnacles. Silver gutta was also used to draw lines on the shells to create the impression of curves.

The sandy background was created by mixing yellow and brown, whilst areas of green and brown were added as seaweed. Salt was used sparingly on the background to give the sand texture. Finally, an impression of a group of pebbles was added using silver and black gutta.

LANDSCAPE: VIEW OF THE VALLEY

Just like sea scenes, so landscapes can be created using little in the way of drawing skills. The wet-on-dry and wet-on-wet techniques detailed on pages 16-17, combined with gutta and sometimes using a careful application of salt, create convincing and evocative landscapes. With any landscape, the skyline and foreground must be composed carefully to lead the viewer into the scene.

In its simplest form, all that is required to create this effective landscape is a blue sky, shades of green for the fields and hills and some details for hedges and trees. Adding a glimpse of yellow flowers gives a focal point. This free experimental way of working is exciting but unpredictable, so it is useful to work on

(Below) Mussel shells, with their flowing lines and delicate sheen, are a lovely subject to paint

(Right) View of the Valley. Landscapes are relatively simple to create, using a few colours and a careful application of gutta

two landscapes at the same time – as one is drying you can add more colour and gutta to the other.

This simple scene looks along a valley towards the sea in the far distance. The hazy blue sky, green fields and trees, together with a field of yellow rape-seed flowers, are created using wet-on-dry, wet-on-wet and gutta techniques.

YOU WILL NEED

masking tape

frame

silk

silk pins

dyes: blue, green, canary yellow and grey

palette

dropper

Chinese paintbrushes

water pot

pipette of colourless gutta

1 Put masking tape on the frame and stretch on the silk using silk pins, as described on page 14.

2 Transfer dyes to the palette with droppers or brushes.

3 Dip a brush in clean water, load with blue to make a pale watery shade and apply a wash of pale blue over the sky area, as would be done with a watercolour. Leave to dry. Rinse the brush clean.

4 Load brush with green and paint the hill line. Along this wet-on-dry line amazing and unexpected shapes appear, giving the impression of trees on the skyline. Rinse the brush clean.

5 Load the brush with canary yellow and apply a strip right across the picture, just below the trees. Leave to dry.

6 Using the pipette of gutta, outline the yellow rape-field area to isolate it. Also outline the distant sea, so that it can be painted pure blue and will not be sullied by invading colours. Leave to dry.

7 Load the brush with green, and paint over the yel-low strip, creating a wet-on-dry effect simulating fields. Whilst this is still wet, apply some blue over the top. Leave to dry.

8 Using the gutta, create the hedgerow and more fields. Leave to dry.

9 Steam and wash, following the instructions given in 'Finishing', page 122.

PIGEONS

One day a racing pigeon came to rest in the studio, and the shimmering turquoise and purple feathers around its neck made it an interesting subject. Sketching a moving bird is not easy, but I was able to jot down various poses and shapes.

YOU WILL NEED

masking tape

frame

silk

silk pins

embroiderer's pen

grey-metallic gutta

dyes: purple, turquoise, grey, black, red and yellow

palette

dropper

Chinese paintbrushes

water pot

paint rag

pipette of colourless gutta

1 Put masking tape on the frame and stretch on the silk using silk pins, as described on page 14.

2 Using an embroiderer's pen, draw the pigeon on the silk.

3 Using grey-metallic gutta, outline the wings and body. Leave to dry.

4 Transfer dyes to the palette using droppers or brushes.

5 Dip a brush in clean water, remove the excess on a paint rag, load with a little purple, and paint the feathers on one side of the neck. Using pale turquoise, repeat this process for the other side of the neck. Leave to dry.

6 Using colourless gutta, draw in some feathers over

Simple though this pigeon painting may seem, it can be very difficult to capture the details of a subject which does not sit still!

Sketching any living creature can be difficult, so try to capture the details on paper

the neck to create a soft feathery effect. Leave to dry.

7 Using deeper shades of turquoise and purple, add more colour over the gutta. Rinse the brush clean.

8 Load brush with pale grey, and paint the rest of the bird, leaving glimmers of white showing on the beak and wing. Paint the shadow under the bird pale grey as well.

9 Using a deep shade of grey, paint the head, wing and tail feathers.

10 Using black, highlight areas on the wing and tail.

11 Paint the legs red, leaving the 'toes' white, and paint the eyes yellow. Leave to dry. Add dots of black for the eyes.

12 Using dark grey, paint over the pale-grey shadow. Lovely dark watermarks will give an interesting sharp edge.

13 Steam and wash, following the instructions given in 'Finishing', page 122.

CAGED BIRDS

The cockatoo panel (right), with its bright colours and interesting shapes, is fairly complex and therefore not really suitable for beginners. However, it uses an interesting and useful technique.

The birds were drawn with gold gutta, the flowers and leaves in grey, colourless and black gutta. The birds were painted in white and yellow, so that they stood out against the background. Some brilliantly coloured

(Above) In Joy Butler's Birdcage *the birds were simplified to create an attractive abstract design*

(Right) Cockatoos painted in a very realistic way

flowers were added to provide spots of colour.

The background blue holds the design together, although it is not one flat colour, but graduates from a pale white/blue at the top to a deep indigo at the

bottom. After it had been finished and steamed, further interest was added by superimposing a silver cage (with open door!) using silver gutta, which only needed iron-fixing.

The second birdcage design, by Joy Butler, illustrates an abstract approach, where the emphasis is more on the pattern created than on the birdcage itself. The design was drawn with bold gutta outlines, using simplified bird shapes which were left pure white, creating the important centre of the design. This was further emphasised by the vivid blue painted around the cage. The colours in the cage echo the colours found in the rest of the design, and gleams of gold applied boldly with a brush around the border add a further dimension (gold gutta or gold Deka fabric paint can be used for this type of effect). The silver stars (or dots) in the sky give the design added light and interest, as does the cleverly broken border.

THE HEDGEROW

An autumn hedgerow was the inspiration for this design. The sketched blackberry leaves and fruit, traveller's joy and honeysuckle needed a sensitive black line which would not run, bleed or leave drops of ink on the silk. In the end (after trial and error), a black waterproof Edding 0.3 pen was used. This design has withstood steaming, washing and ironing and still retains its sketchy feel.

YOU WILL NEED

masking tape

frame

silk

silk pins

Edding 0.3 pen

embroiderer's pen

pipette of colourless gutta

pipette of gold gutta

dyes: pink, blue, grey and green

palette

dropper

Chinese paintbrushes

water pot

paint rag

diluant

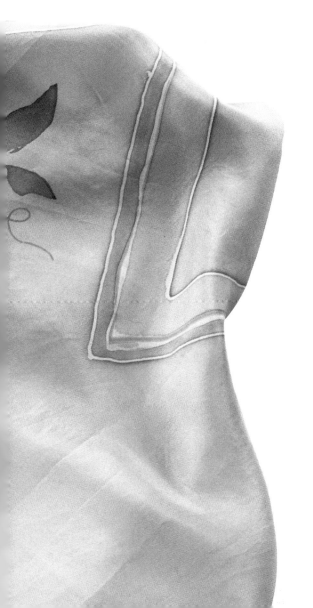

1 Put masking tape on the frame and stretch on the silk using silk pins, as described on page 14.

2 Using an Edding 0.3 pen, sketch the outlines of the blackberry leaves and fruit, traveller's joy and honeysuckle.

3 Using the pipette of colourless gutta, draw over the outlines of the leaves, fruit and flowers, as well as drawing in some white butterflies. To add interest to the final result, do not gutta the black pen line slavishly but sketch freely. Leave to dry.

4 Transfer dyes to the palette using droppers or brushes. Mix some additional colours as required, such as blue and pink, to create deep purple for the blackberries.

5 Dip a brush in clean water, remove the excess on a paint rag, load with deep pink and paint the blackberry flowers. Use a paler shade for the honeysuckle flowers and an even paler shade with some green added for the leaves.

6 Using a pale blue/grey, paint some of the leaves, using a green/blue for the remaining leaves. Paint the blackberries deep purple. Because the pen line is waterproof the colours will not run into each other. Leave to dry.

7 Using the gold gutta, draw round the outlines of the honeysuckle, some of the leaves and along some of the twigs to add 'light'.

8 Mix some grey with diluant to create a very pale grey and use to paint the background.

9 Steam and wash, following the instructions given in 'Finishing', page 122. The finished effect is very much of a watercolour, achieved by using dyes that are well diluted with water to keep the colours soft and imprecise.

NB Various coloured metallic guttas are available and they are excellent for drawing and sketching additional lines and details before or after painting. They leave a positive drawing line and, as they can be superimposed over colours, they can be used to add definition to a piece of work that needs strengthening. Remember to iron before washing.

A sketched effect was used to create this hedgerow design, which was drawn with an Edding waterproof pen

CHAPTER EIGHT

Geometric and Abstract Designs

Geometric shapes and abstract designs are great fun to work. Draw the outlines in bold white or metallic gutta and paint them in startlingly vivid colours for results which shimmer and glow with vibrant life.

Working with geometric shapes and abstract designs is absorbing and fascinating. They are great fun, the completed design can be as simple or as complex as desired, and the results will vary between vibrant and restful, depending on the colours used.

There are four main shapes (devices) which have been used over the centuries: the square, triangle, circle and spiral. Many other devices have been used including floral motifs which were simplified by the Ancient Greeks.

Designs are created by repeating these devices or shapes in various ways to form a 'pattern'. Many old patterns, which at first glance appear to be no more than an abstract design, actually depict animals or birds. Take a look at the illustration showing a thirteenth-century pattern found woven into an Egyptian fabric. At first glance it appears to be a simple abstract pattern, but it is actually made up of formalised bird shapes.

Islamic design shows an amazing knowledge of geometry, used to create exuberant all-over patterns for intricate tiled mosaics. Such patterns, particularly those using the star device, make excellent sources of ideas for silk painting.

Some shapes or devices lend themselves especially to pattern making. They join up in a way that results in exciting shapes being formed, and the use of colour further adds to the excitement of developing these designs. One way to find out which devices are more versatile than others is by experimenting with paper. On some paper, simply draw as many interesting and different shapes you can think of: squares, triangles, stars, S-shapes, paisley shapes, etc, in various sizes. Cut them out and then just play about with them, at first putting together groups of the same shape and size, then combining different sizes and shapes. Working in this way helps you become selective about what does and does not work.

One of my favourite Islamic shapes, which creates many different patterns, is the back-to-front seven. Experiment with it to see what you can create.

An Islamic back-to-front 7 offers great scope for geometric designs

A floral device adopted by the Ancient Greeks

A successful example of geometric shapes used in stripes

Geometric patterns date from ancient times and are often designs of familiar objects, as this formalised bird shows. It was found woven into a fabric dating from the thirteenth century

GEOMETRICS

This is an excellent project for beginners, because there is a limited number of shapes, all easy to create, used in various sizes and combinations. Choose colours that will be vibrant against each other or harmonious together – refer to the colour ladder and colour wheel on pages 37–8. This type of design is a most therapeutic and gentle way of working, as the design gradually emerges as the work progresses.

The zig-zags, triangles and stripes of related shapes in this design were inspired by a visit to Chile, where I was heavily influenced by the traditional woven fabrics in brilliant colours. In the past, such fabrics were dyed with natural dyes made from clay, plants, molluscs, insects, bark and roots. From these materials were created wonderful colours such as indigo, brown, yellow, cochineal, purple and green.

YOU WILL NEED

masking tape

frame

silk: 40cm (16in) square for a cushion, 64cm (25in) square for a scarf

silk pins

colourless gutta

grey-metallic and gold gutta

These zig-zags, triangles and related shapes may be very simple but they can be used to create exciting designs when combined with metallic and plain guttas and vibrant colours

hairdryer

dyes: purple, turquoise, yellow, red, hot pink and black

palette

dropper

Chinese paintbrushes

water pot

paint rag

1 Put masking tape on the frame and stretch on the silk using silk pins, as described on page 14.

2 Using colourless and grey-metallic gutta, draw lines diagonally across the fabric to create stripes of varying widths. Now draw zig-zags and triangles within the stripes, sometimes covering two stripes to create an interesting design. Dry with a hairdryer.

3 Transfer dyes to the palette using droppers or brushes.

4 Load a clean brush with one of the colours and

Two abstract designs by Joy Butler, using simple shapes and positive gutta lines

---

paint between the shapes or inside them. Wash the brush clean, remove the excess water on a paint rag, load with another colour and fill in more shapes and stripes. Continue in this way but leave the outer borders free of colour. Dry.

5 Using colourless and metallic-grey gutta, apply more shapes inside the others.

6 When dry, add more colour, being careful only to add colours that mix with the base colour to produce other exciting shades, for example red over yellow to make orange. Dry.

7 Use gold gutta as a surface decoration, drawing triangles, zig-zags and diamonds as desired. Dry.

8 Load the brush with double-strength black and use to paint the outer borders to show up the rich effect. Dry. Steam and wash, following the instructions given in 'Finishing', page 122. Make up into cushion or scarf.

THE LOTUS SHAPE

This design, based on the lotus bud, is a good shape to develop with the flowing gutta line. It has a simple outline but is very versatile and can be changed in a number of ways to fit all sorts of items, from belts and spectacles cases, to jackets or scarves, as the illustrated examples show. It is a design which also lends itself to being quilted.

When painting the silk for a garment or spectacles case, ensure the paper pattern pieces or template fit comfortably inside the frame on which the silk is stretched. Draw around the template/pattern in gutta before using any dyes, remembering to leave an allowance for seams or turnings.

YOU WILL NEED

masking tape

frame

silk

silk pins

dressmaker's pins

colourless gutta

embroiderer's pen

dyes: pink, red, yellow, blue, black, turquoise and emerald

palette

dropper

Chinese paintbrushes

gold gutta

hairdryer

1 Put masking tape on the frame and stretch on the silk using silk pins, as described on page 14.
2 If used, pin the pattern/template to the silk with dressmaker's pins. Using colourless gutta, draw around the shape allowing for seams/turnings. This stops the dye running unnecessarily. Remove the pattern/template.
3 Using an embroiderer's pen, draw some 'onion' shape outlines all over the silk as a guide.
4 Using colourless gutta, begin in the middle of one of the shapes and start drawing the lotus shape in a continuous line, gradually making it bigger and bigger without taking the pipette off the silk until it is finished. Repeat this process for all the 'onion' shapes on the silk. Dry.
5 Transfer dyes to the palette using droppers or brushes.
6 Load a clean brush with colour and use to fill in part of the shapes.
7 Continue in this way, painting colour within the lotus shapes in any combination. Dry.
8 Once all the shapes have been painted in, colour the background area around them with green, as shown in the spectacles case, or black, as in the waistcoat. Dry.
9 Add more shapes in colourless or gold gutta, and more colour, to create further tones as required. Do not slavishly follow the colours shown in the examples, but create your own colour schemes and experiment with the background colours.
10 Steam and wash, following the instructions given in 'Finishing', page 122. Make up the garment or spectacles case as required.

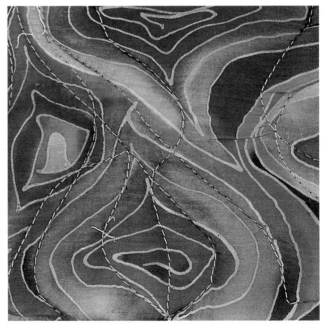

The lotus design lends itself very well to quilting, as the stitching can follow the lotus shape

The lotus shape is an excellent one to use for geometric designs as it can be adapted in a variety of ways, for a spectacles case, collar, or even a waistcoat

CHAPTER NINE

Batik Effect

Batik is a traditional Far Eastern method of using wax and dyes to create beautiful fabric designs.

The true batik process is intricate and lengthy, but it can be adapted and combined with silk painting techniques to produce attractive batik-effect designs.

Batik designs are created by waxing areas of a fabric before immersing the fabric in a dye bath. The waxed areas 'resist' the dye and thus create a pattern. After the fabric has been taken out of the dye, it is left to dry, then the wax is removed. The whole process is repeated for each colour used, making it a lengthy business to produce just one piece of patterned fabric.

When the use of wax is combined with silk painting the whole process is much quicker and gives results which are just as attractive. The process is shortened because the silk dyes are painted on the fabric, rather than the fabric being dipped in a dye bath each time a different colour is required. The combined technique is called batik effect or sneak batik, as it bears very little relationship to the original process used by batik artists. In France it is known as *faux batik*.

Before starting take note of these points.
● Stretch the silk on the frame *before* starting work (applying wax) to prevent the waxed silk sticking to the work surface and spoiling the design. Alternatively, put waxed paper on the work surface. (In Malaya they use banana leaves which have a waxy surface.)
● If hot wax is painted on white silk, the waxed area remains white. Even if colour is painted over the wax the silk stays white.

● Once a colour has been painted on silk, the areas which are to remain that colour are covered with wax before the next colour is applied.

EQUIPMENT AND MATERIALS

silk frame; protected with masking tape

silk painting pins

brushes, preferably hog's hair

batik wax (see below)

wax pot or similar (see below)

tjanting, a special tool for drawing with wax (see below)

newspapers

BRUSHES
Brushes need to withstand being immersed in hot wax. Hog's hair is usually best. When not in use, the brushes should be rested beside the pan on a piece of wood. If left immersed in hot wax, the bristles disintegrate and the brushes fall apart. (When using a wax brush, dip it in the hot wax frequently to ensure the wax stays sufficiently molten to penetrate the silk properly.)

WAX
Special batik wax comes in small pellets and is available from craft shops. It melts easily and, in its molten state, is easy to control. Once dry, it also cracks well, for crackle designs. As an alternative, make a traditional batik wax by melting together $2/3$ paraffin wax to $1/3$ beeswax.

Pure beeswax does not crack at all, so it is unsuitable for crackle designs, although it can be used in a limited way to protect areas of a design that should be kept uncracked. Do not use wax candles or pure paraffin wax, unmixed with beeswax, as they crack and flake off silk very easily.

When wax is applied to silk it must penetrate the fabric, otherwise the fabric is not protected from the dye. Check that this is happening by occasionally holding up the frame to the light. If the cloth is transparent the wax has penetrated. If the wax has not penetrated evenly, apply wax to the reverse side of the silk.

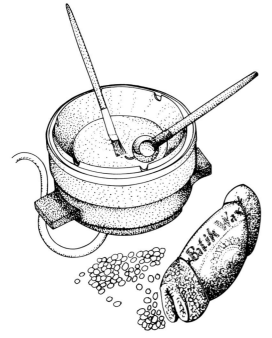

The best way of melting batik wax is in a special thermostatic wax pot which keeps the wax at exactly the right temperature

WAX POT

Wax needs to be melted and heated in a container. There is available a special thermostatic wax pot which keeps the wax at exactly the right temperature, 40°C (104°F), although it is rather expensive.

A double boiler (a pan placed inside another pan containing hot water) is second best – it may be difficult to get the wax to the right temperature and then maintain it (use a sugar thermometer to check temperature). Another option is to use an ordinary thick-based pan, but take special care and have a fire blanket at hand. If wax heats to over 60°C (140°F) it starts smoking, is smelly and dangerous. *Never* leave a pan of molten wax unsupervised – always remove the pan from the heat source before leaving it.

TJANTING

A tjanting is a special metal hand-held tool with a wooden handle and a fire spout. This hole-cum-spout is used to 'draw' the design. Three spout sizes are available: small, medium and large. The largest allows the wax to run out more quickly and makes thick lines, the smallest allows the wax to run out more slowly and makes fine lines. Generally, the hotter the wax, the quicker it flows. It is useful to have a small- and medium-spout tjanting to start with. As wax spreads quickly on silk, practise 'drawing' with the tjanting on newspaper. Just like using gutta, practice is needed to perfect the technique. The secret of success is getting the wax to the right temperature. If the wax is too hot it pours out, making a thick line; if too cold it may flow but not penetrate the silk. Once the correct temperature is achieved, tjanting work is enjoyable and relaxing.

Use a sheet of newspaper folded into a 10cm (4in) square to make a 'drip stopper' for the tjanting – to catch wax dripping from the tjanting as it is applied to and removed from the silk. Newspapers will also be needed to cover the work area.

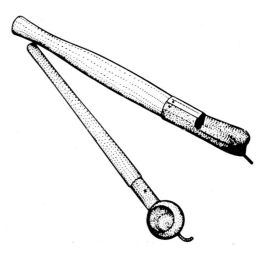

The tjanting is a spouted hand-held tool used for 'drawing' designs in wax

CRACKLE FLOWERS

Crackle, the process of putting cracked colour all over a design, is easy to do and the finished results look most attractive. Any completed silk painting can be given this treatment, although freehand flowers (like those featured on page 55) and landscapes seem to work best.

YOU WILL NEED

silk painting

masking tape

frame

silk pins

batik wax

wax pot or similar

hog's hair wax brush

black silk dye

small container for dye

cotton wool held in a clothes peg, or a paintbrush

kitchen paper

1 Put masking tape on the frame, as described on page 14.

2 Take the silk painting – it can be fixed or unfixed on the silk – and stretch on the frame using silk pins, as described on page 14.

3 Melt wax in the wax pot until it reaches 40°C (104°F).

4 Put the hog's hair brush in the molten wax and leave for a few minutes to warm up. Remove the brush from the wax and paint smoothly over the silk, covering it completely with wax. Frequently dip the brush in the wax pot to ensure it is always loaded with molten wax. Check that the wax has penetrated the silk by holding up the frame to the light to look at the reverse side. If patches of silk remain unwaxed, apply more wax to the back. Batik wax dries almost immediately on application.

5 Remove the silk from the frame and scrunch up in your hands to crack the wax. If it is not cracking well, or if the weather is hot, put the waxed silk into the fridge for about five minutes to cool. Crack again. Hold up the silk to the light to see the result.

6 Stretch the silk back on the frame.

7 Put black dye into a container, dip in a piece of cotton wool held in a clothes peg, or use a paintbrush, and 'paint' over the cracked wax. A scrubbing motion helps the dye get through to the silk.

8 Wipe off any excess dye with a piece of kitchen paper, hold up the silk to the light to see the result. If the dye has not penetrated properly, 'paint' again.

Crackle Flowers

Wipe off excess with kitchen paper. Leave to dry.

9 Iron off the wax, as described on page 125. This also fixes any iron-fix dyes used. Steam-fixed dyes should be ironed to remove the wax then steamed and washed, as described in 'Finishing', page 122.

CRACKLE PIGS

This striking crackle pig design by Angela Newport, shows how wax can be used to keep a background white. The colours were chosen for maximum impact; the stark white background provides an effective contrast to the coloured pigs and green crackle.

YOU WILL NEED

embroiderer's pen

silk

masking tape

frame

silk pins

batik wax

wax pot or similar

6mm (¼in) and 12mm (½in) hog's hair wax brushes

dyes: brown, pink, dark green and dark brown

palette

dropper

Chinese paintbrushes

water pot

paint rag

hairdryer (optional)

cotton wool held in a clothes peg, or paintbrush

kitchen paper

1 Using an embroiderer's pen, draw the pigs on the silk.

2 Put masking tape on the frame and stretch on the silk using silk pins, as described on page 14.

3 Melt wax in the wax pot until it reaches 40°C (104°F).

4 Put the 12mm (½in) hog's hair brush in the molten wax and leave for a few minutes to warm up. Remove the brush from the wax and paint the background of the design, completely covering it with wax. Frequently dip the brush in the wax pot to ensure it is always loaded with molten wax. Check that the wax has penetrated the silk by holding up the frame to the light to look at the reverse side. If patches of silk remain unwaxed, apply more wax to the back.

5 Transfer dyes to the palette using droppers.

6 Dip the paintbrush in clean water, remove the excess on a paint rag, load with brown-pink and paint the pigs. Leave to dry. (Drying with a hairdryer melts the wax, unless a cool setting is used.)

7 Ensure the wax is hot enough, put in the 6mm (¼in) hog's hair brush and leave to warm up for a few minutes. Remove the brush from the wax and paint the pigs with wax, except for their ears, mouths and dots for their eyes. Hold up the frame to the light and look at the reverse side to check that the wax has come through.

8 Using dark-brown dye, paint over the pigs' ears, mouths and eyes. Wipe off any excess with kitchen paper. Leave to dry. Wax over the dark brown areas.

9 Remove the silk from the frame and scrunch up in your hands so that the wax cracks. If it is not cracking well, or if the weather is hot, cool the waxed silk in the fridge for about five minutes. Crack again.

10 Stretch the silk back on the frame.

11 Put dark-green dye into the palette, dip in a piece of cotton wool held in a clothes peg, or a paintbrush, and 'paint' over the wax on both sides using a scrubbing motion.

12 Wipe off any excess dye with a piece of kitchen paper, hold up the silk to the light to see the result. If the dye has not penetrated properly, paint again. Wipe off excess with kitchen paper. Leave to dry.

13 Iron off the wax, steam and wash, as described in 'Finishing', page 122.

Crackle Pigs *by Angela Newport makes good use of contrasting colours*

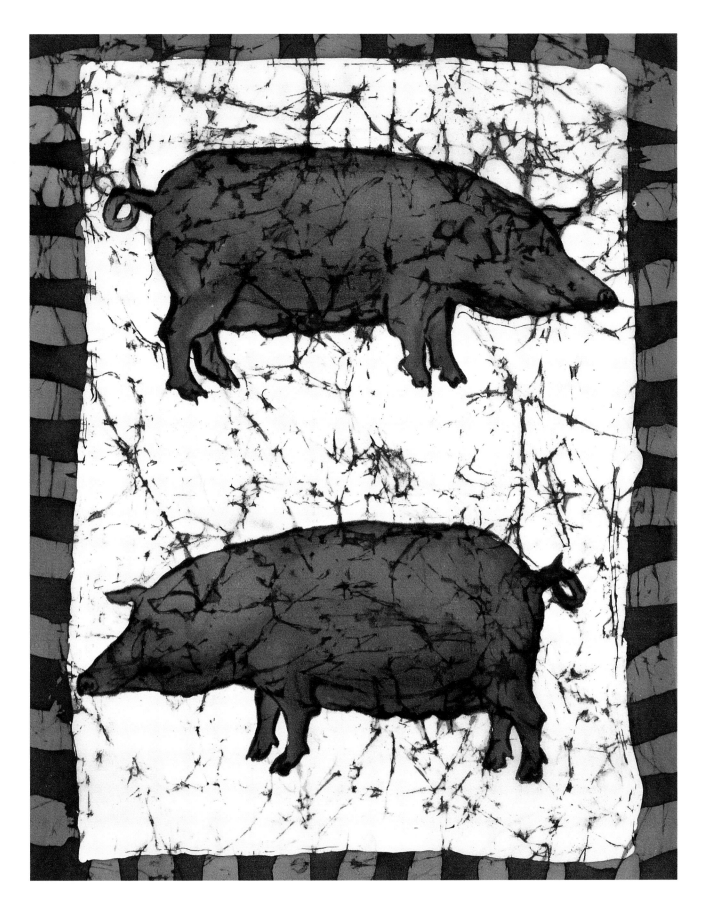

WAX FLOWER SCARF

This lovely design, created by Jill Castor, illustrates a free way of working with wax and colour. Areas of colour were painted on the silk – using the wet-meeting-wet technique – and thoroughly dried. The detailed floral design was 'drawn' using hot wax and brushes, then more colour was added on top. It is an enjoyable project to do, provided you remember which colours work on top of one another and which ones do not (refer back to the colour ladder and wheel on pages 37-8).

Creating such an intricate wax design requires good control of the tjanting, which comes with prac-tice. One of the tricks is to have a drip stopper always at hand to prevent drips of wax getting on the work. This happens when the tjanting is removed from the wax pot, so hold a piece of newspaper under the spout, to catch the drops of wax. Begin drawing with the liquid wax, first letting it run on the paper before moving it onto the silk, catching any drips with the newspaper stopper. Always move the newspaper under the spout before the tjanting is replaced in the wax pot.

Wax Flower Scarf by Jill Castor, created with the tjanting

YOU WILL NEED

masking tape

frame

90cm (35in) quare silk scarf

silk pins

newspapers

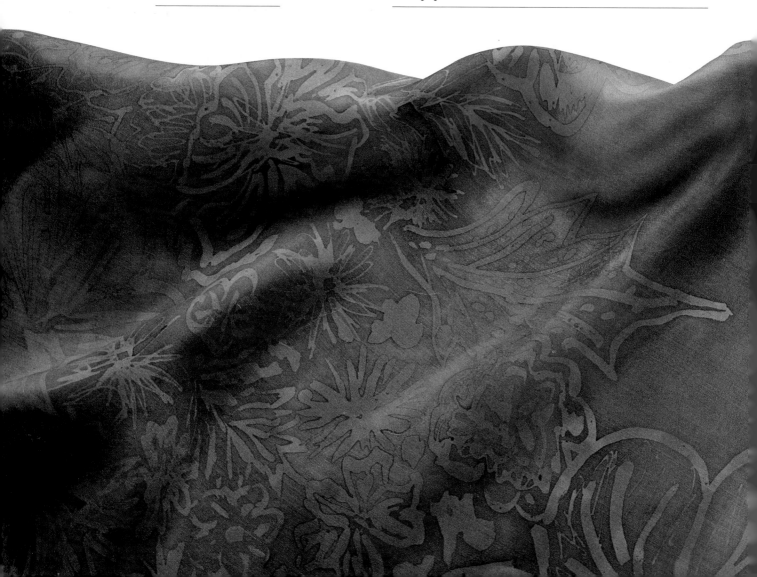

steam-fixed dyes: pink, turquoise, soft red, purple, yellow and blue

dropper

palette

water pot

paint rag

Chinese paintbrushes

hairdryer

batik wax

wax pot or similar

6mm (¼in) hog's hair wax brush

tjanting with medium spout

drip stopper

1 Put masking tape on the frame and stretch on the silk using silk pins, as described on page 14. Cover the work area with newspaper.

2 Transfer dyes to the palette using droppers.

3 Dip a brush in clean water, remove the excess on a paint rag, load with pink and use to paint areas of the silk. Rinse the brush clean.

4 Repeat this process using turquoise, soft red and purple, so that the silk is completely covered by colour. Dry with a hairdryer. Wax does not penetrate a damp cloth.

5 Melt wax in the wax pot until it reaches 40°C (104°F). Put in the tjanting to warm up.

6 Practise the flow of the tjanting on the newspaper, making sure the wax is near at hand, but safely positioned. Take the tjanting out of the wax and rest the spout on the drip stopper. Run off the drip stopper onto the newspaper and, with the end of the spout touching the paper, lightly draw circles and lines to see how freely or slowly the line is made (this

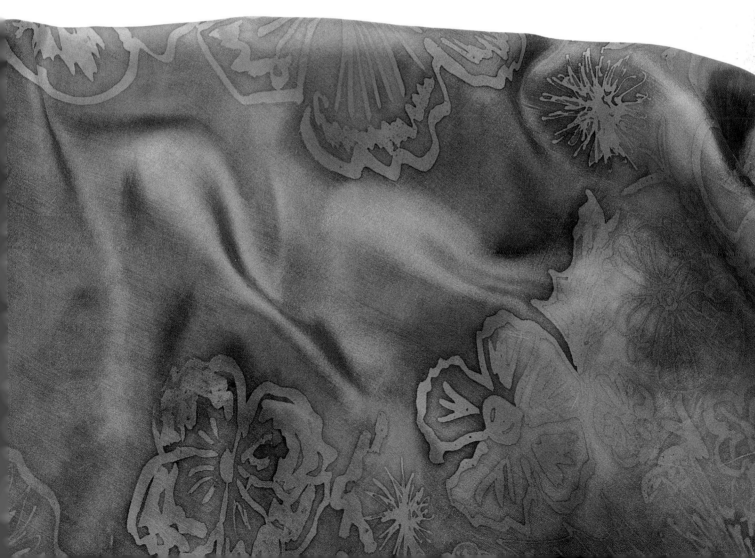

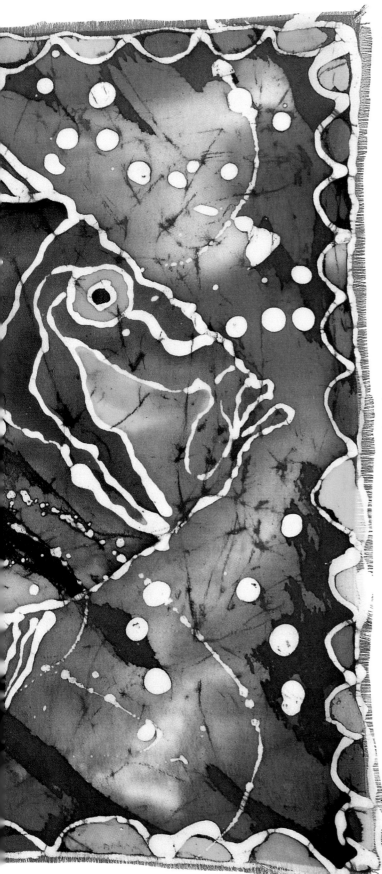

depends on the heat of the wax and size of the spout). When the wax is flowing freely, start drawing on the silk, remembering to use the drip stopper before running on or off the fabric.

7 Continue the tjanting work, then use the hog's hair brush to complete the design, frequently dipping it in the wax pot to ensure the wax stays molten.

8 Once the wax design is complete – it dries almost immediately – paint over more colour. This is an exciting time because, although the colours underneath the wax remain intact, the unwaxed colours change. Apply yellow freely over blue, purple, red and pink turning turquoise to bright green, pink to purple, red to orange. Knowing what happens when certain colours are painted over one another makes this an enjoyable task. Leave to dry.

9 Iron off the wax, steam and wash, as described in 'Finishing', page 122.

BATIK EFFECT FISH

Angela Newport's free style of painting with wax is especially suited to using a tjanting, as seen with this batik-effect design. The fish outline was drawn in wax with a tjanting, although Angela did not use a drip stopper, but allowed the wax to drip in an exaggerated way, using the drops to add 'movement' to the design.

After the outline had been completed, the fish was painted in red, yellow and blue merging dyes. Note the way these colours have been used: making a turquoise eye with a hint of purple; graduating the red to orange in the body; mixing yellow and blue to create a green belly. In contrast, the background was painted in shades of blue, with some areas over painted green to make turquoise.

Once the dyes had dried, the entire work was painted from corner to corner, with broad brush strokes of hot wax in one direction only, while some parts of the silk were intentionally left unwaxed. The silk was then cracked and black dye painted over the design, emphasising the direction of the final wax brush strokes.

Angela Newport's Fish *makes a feature of the drips of wax from the tjanting*

CHAPTER TEN

Marbling

Marbling on silk is great fun and much easier than most people imagine. Even complete beginners can produce beautiful effects with very little effort. The materials, which are readily available, are not messy to use and the dyes used here are all water based. Anyone can marble on silk and use the technique to make scarves, picture panels, fabric cards, cushion covers and ties. Larger pieces of silk can be marbled and then used to make up camisole tops or waistcoats.

The principle of marbling is to float colours on a liquid base, which is thick enough for the colours not to sink and viscous enough for the colours to be moved into a controllable pattern. This base is called size.

When marbling, it is helpful to have another pair of hands to help when handling large pieces of fabric. In fact, marbling is an excellent group activity, as large baths of size can be made and used again and again. Although the same size is used, individuals can choose their own colours and create their own designs. Special marbling equipment is available from good art and craft shops, but equally good results can be achieved using home-made equipment.

EQUIPMENT AND MATERIALS

a bath or trough

polystyrene meat trays

size (foundation)

mordant (alum)

oxgall

combs, cocktail sticks, satay sticks and needles

marbling colours

silk

newspaper

plastic spoons

Beautiful marbled scarves

BATH OR TROUGH

A professional marbling trough is usually made of metal with a storage section at one end for the size, colours and paper. It is not necessary to have a rigid trough, but it is advisable to make one that can adapt to different dimensions

A home-made trough can be constructed from four lengths of wood, each 5–7cm (2–3in) deep, laid on a work surface and overlapping at the corners to make the required dimensions for, say, a scarf. Put a thick sheet of transparent plastic over the top, push-ing it down to the work surface and into the corners to form a trough, then pin or staple to the wood. This holds the wood in place. It is now ready for the size to be poured in.

SIZE (FOUNDATION)

Size, or foundation, is the liquid base which must be thick enough to hold colours on top, yet fluid enough to allow the colours to be moved into a pattern and

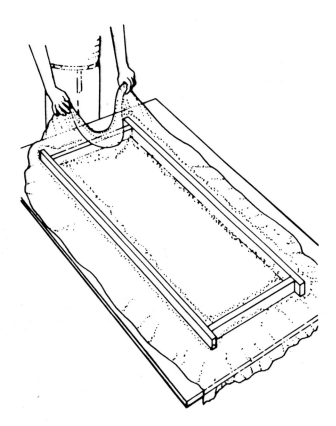

A marbling trough can be made by putting four lengths of wood together to form a rectangle, putting a sheet of heavy-duty plastic in the well, and pinning or stapling in place

Size Recipe 1 – Carrageen Moss Powder

Mix one tablespoon of powdered moss with 300ml (½pt) hot rainwater in a blender or liquidiser, or use a hand whisk. Mix for 30 seconds or until smooth, then add 1 litre (1¾pt) cold rainwater.

The result is a rather slimy clear light-brown liquid. Put this in a bucket and leave covered in a cool place for twelve hours, stirring occasionally. Pour gently into the trough, trying to avoid air bubbles as these need to be burst before work commences.

This is the easiest and least smelly way of mixing size, but it is a little more expensive than the next recipe.

then stay put. Some manufacturers, such as Deka, Javana, Delta and Pebéo, make a marbling medium suitable for use with their own (and other manufacturers') dyes. A more economical method, particularly for making large quantities, is to make your own size using one of the recipes given below.

Carrageen moss (an Irish seaweed), provides the best foundation for floating colours, although it is sensitive to temperature variations, going thinner when warm and thicker when cool. It goes off after a few days and a size preservative can be added to prolong its life. Mix with rainwater or distilled water for the best results, although adding water softener to tap water works reasonably well too. Tap water alone may contain excessive minerals which affect the size and, although it can be adjusted, beginners may find it a bit too difficult to achieve the right balance.

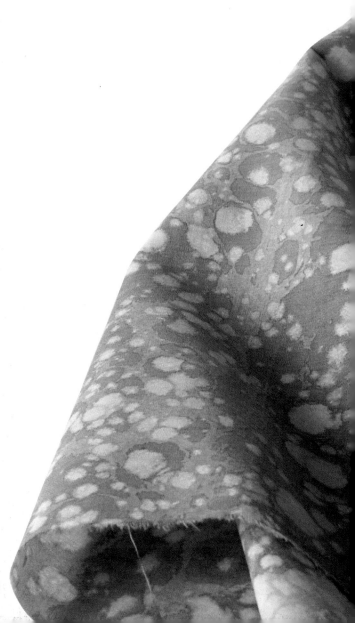

Size Recipe 2 – Dried Carrageen Moss

Bring 4 litres (7pt) rainwater to the boil. Add 25g (1oz) dried carrageen moss and boil for five minutes, stirring with a stick (do not allow to boil over). Remove from the heat, stir in 0.5 litre (¾pt) cold rainwater and leave to stand in a cool place for twelve hours. Strain through a cloth such as muslin, into a bucket. The cloth should not be squeezed and, as this process can take an hour or so, you will need to set up a hook or upturned stool to hang the cloth from.

MORDANT

Silk must be dipped in mordant prior to being marbled so that the colours will adhere to it. Mordant can be made cheaply using alum powder, which is available from chemists. (Buy a small quantity just before using it, as alum does not keep well.)

Use marbling to make lampshades and fabrics

To make the mordant, mix one tablespoon of alum with 600ml (1pt) heated rainwater. When the crystals have disappeared, pour the mixture into a screw-top jar – it will keep for a few weeks. If the crystals re-form, pour the mordant into a pan and heat gently. (Take care not to inhale the fumes.)

OXGALL

If the dyes do not spread well on the size, a few drops of oxgall added to the dyes acts as a dispersing agent to reduce surface tension and allow the colours to expand on the surface. For convenience, buy ready-made oxgall from art shops. Although it *can* be made at home using neat oxgall and gin, this is a disgusting process and not to be recommended!

COMBS, COCKTAIL STICKS, SATAY STICKS AND NEEDLES

Various implements, such as combs, cocktail sticks, satay sticks and knitting needles, can be used to draw patterns in the colours. A home-made comb can be made by hammering nails, equal distances apart, into a length of wood, then breaking off the heads using a pair of pliers (see drawing).

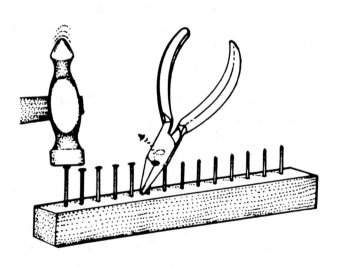

Make a marbling comb by hammering nails in a piece of wood, an equal distance apart, then break off the nail heads with a pair of pliers

COLOURS

The dyes used for marbling include gouache (more commonly used for watercolours), iron-fixed silk dyes and special marbling colours. All are available from art shops.

SILK

Any type of natural fibre, including silk and silk/cotton mixtures, is suitable for marbling. Avoid imitation silks and artificial fabrics which may reject the dyes.

NEWSPAPERS

Dust particles can lie on the surface of the size bath. Also, if the size is left to stand for a few hours, a 'skin' can form. Both of these problems will mar the finished result, so it is a good idea to skim the surface of the size before you start. The easiest way to do this is to use newspaper.

Gently drag a strip of newspaper over the surface of the size bath from one end to the other; then throw away the paper. This method removes any leftover surface colour together with any dirt and dust. (Repeat until the surface is completely clean.)

HOW TO MARBLE

Initially, it is worth practising the marbling techniques using polystyrene meat trays (the type you buy pre-packed meat in at supermarkets). Put small quantities of size in the trays, add the dyes, create the patterns and use a small piece of fabric which has been mordanted to see that the size is of the right consistency and that the finished design is satisfactory.

1 Mix the size the night before, using one of the recipes given.

2 Soak silk in the alum mixture (mordant) for five minutes. Wearing rubber gloves, remove the silk, squeeze out excess liquid gently and hang the silk up to dry. Iron lightly and tear to fit the practice marbling tray.

3 Stir the size well and pour some into three polystyrene meat trays.

4 Open a bottle of dye and stir thoroughly with a cocktail or satay stick. *Gently* touch the surface of the

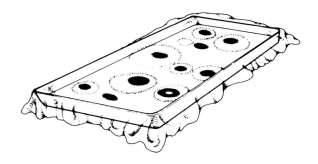

Apply drops of dye to the surface of the bath, starting with the pale colours

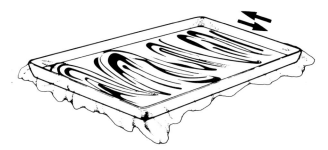

Lightly pass a toothpick across the surface of the dyes in the size bath to produce a pattern

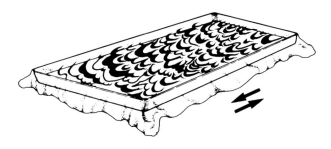

A comb passed lengthwise over the surface creates an interesting pattern

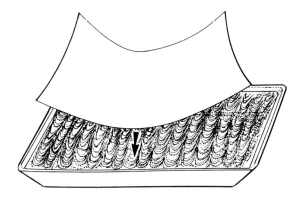

Once the design has been created on the size, place the silk carefully on the surface, centre first to avoid trapping any air, and leave for five seconds

size in one of the trays with the stick of dye and see how well the dye spreads. The colour should spread in a circle.

5 If it does not spread well, add a little rainwater to the size in the second tray and mix. Add another circle of dye with the stick.

6 If the colour still refuses to spread, the dye may be too thick. Add a few drops of rainwater or oxgall to the dye, mix with a stick. Gently touch the surface of the size with the stick of dye to create another circle.

7 These tests should show what remedial action – if any – is needed to obtain good results: either changing the size consistency before putting it into the bath, or altering the consistency of the dye. Once this has been done, carefully pour size into the bath to prevent air bubbles forming.

8 Starting with the lightest colour, stir the dye with a stick. *Gently* touch the surface of the size with the stick of dye, allowing it to form a small circle. Repeat, applying as many circles of colour as required. Always *gently* touch the surface to apply the colour, *never* drop it from a height or it will drop from the surface to the bottom of the bath, where it will be no use at all.

9 Repeat with the other chosen colours, working from the lightest to the darkest. The surface will now be covered in circles of different colours.

10 Carefully pass a stick, knitting needle or comb, over the surface of the size to produce a pattern. Do this slowly so that no air bubbles are formed.

11 Lay a piece of alum-treated silk on the surface, centre first to avoid trapping any air underneath. Make sure all the fabric is in contact with the surface of the bath. Leave for five seconds. The dyes are now fixed to the silk fibres and colourfast. (If alum had not been used the colours would just wash off.)

12 Lift out the silk carefully, holding each end, let it drip, rinse under a gentle flow of cold water and peg on a line to dry.

13 The surface of the bath should be completely clean and the entire pattern should have transferred to the silk. Skim the surface clean with newspaper, as described above. The size can now be used to create another pattern.

14 Once the silk has dried, squeeze it gently in warm, soapy water, and hang up to dry. Iron lightly.

CREATING DESIGNS

The following examples show how to create different marbling designs.

A

1 Dip the silk in alum, leave for five minutes, take out. Squeeze gently, hang up to dry, iron lightly.

2 Using a cocktail or satay stick, apply circles of orange, blue and green dye to the surface of the size bath.

3 Pass stick up and down through the dyes, drawing the colours gently into shapes. No more work is needed as the dye remains in solid blocks of colour.

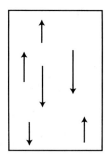

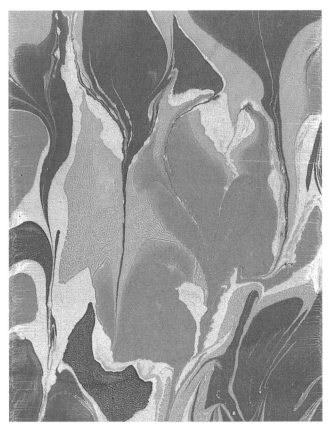

B

1 Dip the silk in alum, leave for five minutes, take out. Squeeze the silk gently, hang up to dry and iron lightly.

2 Using a cocktail or satay stick, apply circles of white, yellow, purple and red dye, in that order, to the surface of the size bath.

3 (a) Pass the stick, in a continuous straight zig-zag movement, working from top to bottom of the bath, passing through the circles of dye.

4 (b) With the same stick, use single straight lines, moving up from side to side of the bath.

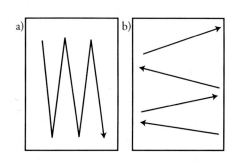

C

This silk was untreated with alum because gouache was used and this adheres well to silk.

1 In three separate cups squeeze out 12mm (½in) of white, pink and blue gouache from their tubes. Using plastic spoons, mix each one with a little water until they are a creamy consistency.

2 Using a cocktail or satay stick, apply circles of white, pink and blue dye, in that order, to the surface of the size bath.

3 (a) With the stick, make circular swirls of movement so that the arcs of the swirls face the top and bottom of the bath.

4 (b) With the same stick, make single straight lines from end to end of the bath.

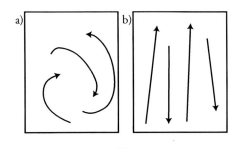

D

Like design C, the silk was untreated with alum because gouache was used. However, shades of pale blue appeared in the design because the colour had been left on the size from the previous example (design C). The finished result is not unpleasant, but it does show how important it is to skim the bath after each design to avoid any disastrous results.

1 Squeeze out 12mm (½in) of pink gouache from the tube into a cup. Using a plastic spoon, mix with a little water until it is a creamy consistency.

2 Using a cocktail or satay stick, apply circles of dye to the surface of the size bath.

3 (a) With the stick, work in single straight lines across the bath.

4 (b) Make circular swirls of movement.

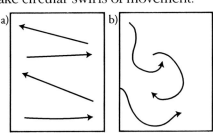

117

E

1 Dip the silk in alum, leave for five minutes, take out. Squeeze the silk gently, hang up to dry and iron lightly.

2 (a) Using a cocktail or satay stick, apply large circles of yellow, pink and blue dyes, in that order, to the surface of the size bath.

3 (b) Using the stick, make single straight lines working from top to bottom of the bath.

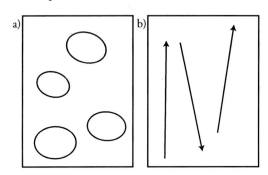

F

1 Dip the silk in alum, leave for five minutes, take out. Squeeze the silk gently, hang up to dry and iron lightly.

2 Using a cocktail or satay stick, apply circles of yellow, pink and blue dye in that order, to the surface of the size bath.

3 (a) With the stick, work in single straight lines across the bath, moving up from bottom to top, then down.

4 (b) With a continuous straight top to bottom zig-zag movement.

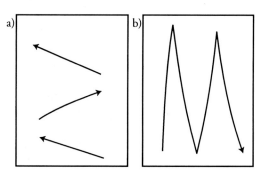

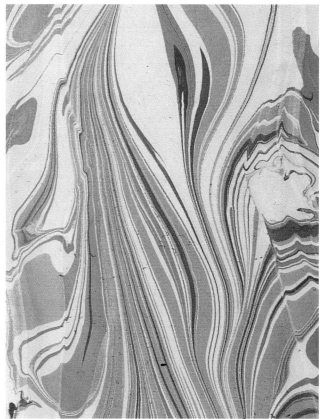

G

1 Dip the silk in alum, leave for five minutes, take out. Squeeze the silk gently, hang up to dry and iron lightly.

2 Using a cocktail or satay stick, apply circles of white and pale-blue dye in that order, to the surface of the size bath.

3 (a) Using the stick, apply more circles of dye on top of the others, first pink then white then dark blue and finally a small dot of white in the centre.

4 (b) Using the stick, carefully create flower shapes, always working from the outside edge of the coloured circles inwards towards the centres.

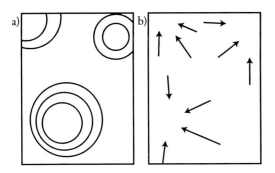

H

1 This design follows the same procedure as design G, up to and including step 3, where circles of dye are applied on top of one another.

2 (b) Using a cocktail or satay stick, instead of creating flower shapes by working from the outside edge of the coloured circles and going inwards, start from the *centre* of the circles and work *outwards* in slightly curved lines.

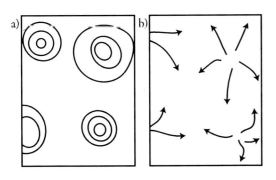

SOLVING PROBLEMS

These three examples show some of the effects which may occur if the materials are not suitably prepared, and explain how to correct them.

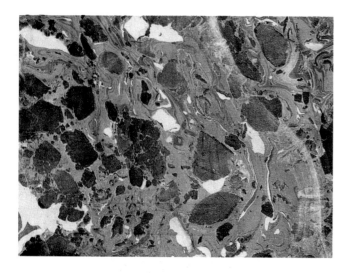

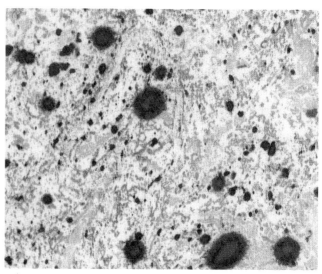

• Total failure here as the colours are not spreading at all.

Solution: the size is probably too thick and should be diluted with a little distilled water or rainwater.

• The colours break up on the surface instead of forming attractive swirls.

Solution: add a few drops of oxgall or water to the dyes. If this does not help, there is likely to be a chemical in the bath. Skimming may help – if not, throw away the size and wash all the equipment thoroughly before starting again.

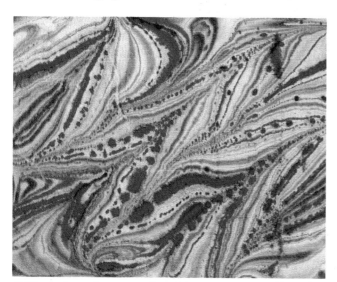

• Here the colours are breaking up into small circles rather than moving about smoothly.

Solution: add a little oxgall or water to the dyes to make them expand on the surface. Skimming the surface will help as dust may be present.

CHAPTER ELEVEN

FINISHING

Any silk painting created with steam-fixed dyes must be steamed to bring out the glorious vibrant colours. It is not a complicated or difficult process, although it must be done carefully otherwise the painting could end up a soggy watermarked piece of work. There is no mystique to the process. Paintings can easily be steamed in the kitchen without using any special equipment, although they must be completely dry before they are steamed and must be kept well away from water until after the dyes have been fixed.

STEAMING SILK

EQUIPMENT AND MATERIALS

large base pan for the water

newspapers

masking tape

roll of tinfoil

spoon

lidded steamer
(28cm (11in) across
is a good size)

Use a large, 28cm (11in) diameter, lidded steamer to steam the silk

1 Fill pan half-full with water and bring to the boil.
2 Wrap the finished work lightly in newspaper – to avoid creasing – following the diagrams. Secure roll with a small piece of masking tape. (Sellotape is no good as it attracts moisture, as do rubber bands and string.)

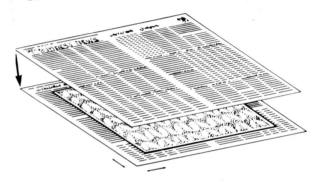

Place the silk painting to be steamed between single sheets of newspaper, to form a 'sandwich'; smooth down

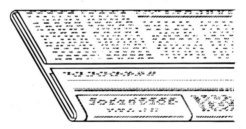

Take one of the longer edges of the newspaper sandwich and fold it into the centre, repeat with the second edge so that the two long edges meet at the centre of the paper

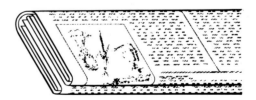

Fold the paper in half lengthways at the point at which the two edges meet

FINISHING AT A GLANCE

DYES	
steam-fixed	steam then wash
iron-fixed	iron then wash
steam-fixed & iron-fixed (used separately)	steam-fixed dyes can be used first, then fixed by steaming iron-fixed dyes can be used over the original design, then ironed to finish the work
GUTTA water-based	washes out after steaming or ironing
spirit-based	washes out after steaming or ironing – if stubborn, soak in white spirit for five minutes then wash again. If steamed too long they are more difficult to remove.
metallic	iron then wash
WAX AND . . . iron-fixed dyes	iron to remove wax (the dye is fixed at the same time)
steam-fixed dyes	iron to remove wax, then steam, then wash

Fold the paper in half lengthways to form a long roll

Turn in the ends and fold the roll from either end. Keep together with a small piece of masking tape

Place the rolled parcel on a large piece of tinfoil

3 Lay the newspaper roll on a large piece of tinfoil and crumple the edges of the tinfoil as shown in the diagram. Wrap around the newspaper roll, leaving an opening at the top to let in the steam.

4 Put an upturned spoon on the bottom of the steamer and place the tinfoil package on top of it *with the opening facing downwards*. The spoon, together

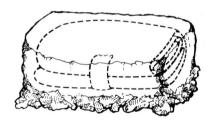

Wrap the tinfoil around the paper parcel

Leave the bottom of the tinfoil parcel open to let in the steam. Crumple the edge to keep it off the base of the steamer

Place the tinfoil parcel in the steamer, open side down, on an upturned spoon so that the parcel does not come into contact with any water which may gather on the base of the steamer

with the crumpled tinfoil edge, will keep the package off the base of the steamer where water may gather.

5 Put the steamer, with the lid on, over the boiling water and steam gently, for forty to sixty minutes.

6 Remove from the steamer, undo parcel and take out a glorious vibrant piece of silk. Leave the silk overnight if possible to allow the dyes to settle, then wash following the instructions given on page 125.

RULES FOR SUCCESS

● *Never* use a piece of tinfoil twice. This might seem extravagant, but it is necessary. If you hold a piece of used tinfoil up to the light after steaming, you will see it is full of tiny pinpricks. If it is used again these holes will let moisture through and ruin the work.

●Watch the water level in the pan. If the pan boils dry the paper could catch fire and ruin your work of art. (This might sound incredible, but I have seen it happen.)

● Use single layers of newspaper to wrap up the silk and use as little paper as possible; too much prevents steam penetrating thoroughly and evenly.

● Use good-quality newspapers without any colour printing. They should be a few weeks old, otherwise the fresh print may come off onto the work.

● Practise folding the parcels, following the given illustrations, until it becomes second nature.

● Always use a large steamer which allows the steam to circulate right around the parcel. If the lid is forced down on top of the parcel, it might push a corner of it into some water.

LARGER STEAMERS

A small steamer is perfectly suitable for single items and for small pieces of silk. It will not be adequate for large items or if there is a lot of work to steam. Large rectangular steamers – which resemble fish kettles – are available from good craft shops. Always make sure these large containers will fit over two rings on your hob so that the water boils evenly to generate the steam.

With these steamers, the silk is placed on a single sheet of newspaper and the two are rolled around and around a wooden pole, layer upon layer; this enables several metres to be rolled around the wood for one steaming. When all the silk has been rolled on, fix the paper in place with small pieces of masking tape to prevent it unrolling. Place the roll in the holders in the steamer so that it is suspended over the boiling water, put on the lid. Leave to steam for about an hour for up to four scarves, and one-and-a-half to two hours for long lengths. The required time

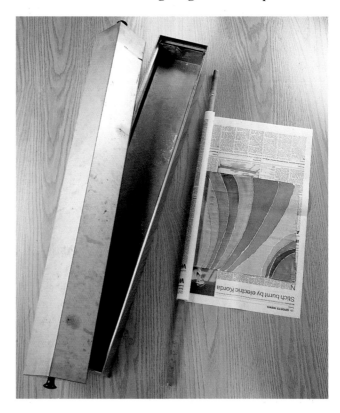

Large steamer suitable for steaming several paintings at a time. Roll the painting in newspaper around the roller before putting into the steamer

depends on how much silk is wrapped on the roll. If a few metres of thicker silk have to be penetrated by the steam it should be left for two hours. Check the water level hourly so that the pan does not boil dry.

Another, but more costly, option is to buy an upright thermostatically controlled steamer from a good craft shop.

WHEN THINGS GO WRONG

Sometimes steaming can go wrong – if the tinfoil has holes in it, for example, or if the water penetrates through to the silk. Take heart, as the work is not always totally lost. Look at the design and work out how it can be redone. Add new gutta and more colour over the original and steam again, taking great care to do things properly this time. You may be surprised at the result.

The floral design shown overleaf was supposed to be brilliantly coloured nasturtium heads against a beautiful pale blue-grey background. Steaming with second-hand tinfoil resulted in a messy, blotchy, watermarked work and the pale background was ruined. (So, remember, *never* use tinfoil twice!)

To save the design, it was re-worked with more gutta and colour. A stronger background was created and additional colour painted over the nasturtiums. Because the original colours had been steamed they did not move when the new colours were added and, after a second (successful) steaming, this rich design was the result.

IRON-FIXED DYES

If iron-fixed dyes have been used it is important to fix them before the silk is washed. This is very easily done. Set an iron to a medium setting, then iron the back of the silk for about three minutes, moving the iron around all the time. The dyes will now be set and the silk can be washed.

WASHING SILK PAINTING

Once the dyes have been fixed leave the silk for a couple of days to allow the colours to settle, then it is ready to be washed, as follows:

1 Use hand-hot water with a gentle non-detergent soap. (The type used for washing woollens is per-fect.) It should not contain any enzymes or alkalis, which bleach and damage the silk, and possibly the dyes as well.

2 Rinse the silk in warm or cold water and hang to dry.

3 Iron whilst still damp for the best results.

Washing Tips

• If dye washes out, it is usually only the excess that the fibres were unable to absorb during fixing. If a great amount of dye washes out, it has not been steamed for long enough.

• If spirit gutta has not washed out, it was too thickly applied in the first place, or it was over-steamed. Soak the silk in white spirit for five minutes; the gutta will then turn to a jelly-like consistency and can be removed by gentle rubbing or by scraping off with a fingernail. Wash again in warm soapy water.

• Water-based gutta should wash out easily, but if it has been steamed for over an hour it may not come off properly. Soak the silk in warm soapy water for five minutes, then gently rub off.

• Metallic guttas need to be ironed *before* washing so remember the order: (1) steam, (2) iron and (3) wash.

• If the gutta is not thoroughly dry before steaming (it is best left overnight), newspaper print often adheres to it during the steaming process. Do not worry. Wash in the ordinary way, and the newsprint will come off easily. Metallic guttas must be iron-fixed after steaming but *before* washing.

REMOVING BATIK WAX

It takes a little thought when using wax to remember how and when to fix the dyes. Follow these few simple guidelines to achieve the correct finished result:

• Whatever dyes are used, always remove the wax first by ironing. Do this by putting about a dozen layers of newspaper on an ironing board. Lay the waxed silk on them and place a single sheet of newspaper over it. Use a medium-hot iron and iron over the waxed silk. As the single sheet of paper becomes saturated with wax, remove it, as well as the one underneath the silk. Put another sheet of newspaper on top and repeat the process until all wax has been removed and the newspaper remains clean.

• If iron-fixed dyes and metallic guttas have been used, they are fixed by the ironing.

• If steam-fixed dyes have been used, follow the procedure described for steaming silk, on page 122.

• After steaming, wash in warm soapy water to remove the last of the wax and surplus dye. Rinse in cold water.

• After all the fixing processes have been completed you may still feel some wax in the silk. To remove it

The original Nasturtiums *was ruined by water getting onto the silk. The design was reworked to create this successful result*

put some white spirit in a bowl and immerse the silk in it. Leave for five minutes, take out and hang up. The wax should all have gone and the smell of the white spirit will disappear naturally, although you can wash the silk in warm, soapy water if you prefer.

DYES AND SUPPLIERS

INTERNATIONAL DYE EQUIVALENTS

	STEAM FIX	IRON FIX	MARBLING
AUSTRALIA	Dupont Sennelier	Deka	Pebéo
FRANCE	Pebéo Sennelier	Seta Color Deka	Pebéo
GERMANY	Uhlig	Javana	Hobidée
UK	Kniazeff Dupont	Seta Colour Javana Deka	Pebéo Javana
USA	Dupont	Deka	Delta (Marblefix) Deka

DYE SUPPLIERS

AUSTRALIA
Octovo Pty Ltd, PO Box 324, Coogee, NSW 2034

FRANCE
Pousard Frères, 28 rue du Sentier, 75002 Paris

GERMANY
Gallery Smend, Mainze Strasse 31, Postfach 250360, 5000 Köln
Hobbidée (Marbling colours), Turbinstrasse 7, 7600 Stuttgart 31

UK
George Weil & Son Ltd, Reading Arch Road, Redhill, Surrey (or 18 Hanson Street, London W1)
Candle Makers Suppliers, 28 Blythe Road, London W14

USA
Cerulean Blue Ltd, PO Box 21168, Seattle, Washington 08111
Dhasma Trading Co, PO Box 150916, San Rafael, California 94915

ACKNOWLEDGEMENTS

Many people have provided invaluable help during the creation of this book. My thanks to Jill Caster, William Weil, Alan Hebden, Celia Buchanan, J. & J., Edda Aschmann, Vivienne Wells, Ethan Danielson, Guy Venables, West Dean College, Solveig Stone of Compton Marbling, Tisbury, Wilts and the following designers who have contributed pieces of work: Angela Newport, No 4, Woodleaze, Seamills, Bristol BS9 2HY; John Farmelo, 15 Tower Road, Worthing, West Sussex BN11 1DP; Joy Butler, ISAF Design Ltd, Cefn Isa, Cilcain, Mold, Clwyd CH7 5NS, Wales; Frannie, Basement Studios, 7 New Cavendish Street, London W1; and Katherine Korrell.

The author is available for commissions and can be contacted at Windmill Cottage, Stoughton, Chichester, West Sussex PO18 9JJ.

INDEX

Page numbers in *italic* indicate illustrations